Classic Restaurants of LOUISVILLE

Classic Restaurants OF LOUISVILLE

STEPHEN HACKER

Published by American Palate
A Division of The History Press
Charleston, SC 29403
www.historypress.net

Front cover, top left: courtesy John Nation; *top center*: courtesy Dan Dry/*Food & Dining Magazine*; *top right*: courtesy John Nation; *bottom left*: courtesy Michael Johmann; *bottom right*: courtesy John Nation.
Back cover: courtesy the Jones family; *left inset*: courtesy Druther's Systems; *right inset*: courtesy Dan Dry/*Food & Dining Magazine*.

First published 2020

Manufactured in the United States

ISBN 9781467144964

Library of Congress Control Number: 2020941859

Notice: The information in this book is true and complete to the best of our knowledge. It is offered without guarantee on the part of the author or The History Press. The author and The History Press disclaim all liability in connection with the use of this book.

For Buffy, who is very fond of restaurants. And for Michelle, whose intelligence and patience make me a much better writer and person.

Contents

Acknowledgments

I am grateful to Michael Johmann, John Nation, Dan Dry, John Carlos White, Stephen Jones, Luckett Davidson, Joe Bonura, Greg Haynes, Brian Easley, Bim Deitrich, William Faversham, John Shaver and many others who shared their time, photographs, stories and memorabilia.

Introduction

Every restaurant has a story. Each represents an idea. An invitation. An organization of chefs, servers, dishwashers and delivery people who try and stand out in a crowded arena. Many don't make it. But some, even though their time may have been brief, created meals and memories that last through many years. As in my previous book, *Lost Restaurants of Louisville*, the restaurants in this volume are special to many people around the city—and, I hope, even to those unfamiliar with Dirty Min's or Queenie Bee.

1

732 Social

CRAFT COCKTAIL, COMMUNAL SEATING AND ENVIRONMENTAL CONSCIOUSNESS

With Basa Modern Vietnamese, Steven and Michael Ton gave Louisville an elegant avenue to explore Southeast Asian ideas. Their next project was a restaurant that would work as part of an artistic and environmental collective. "There is a cultural revolution happening here," Gill Holland declared to the *New York Times* in 2008. The cornerstone of the plans that Holland and his wife, Augusta Brown Holland, had for "Louisville's hip but slightly depressed East Market Street area" known as NuLu was converting a century-old warehouse into an energy- and environmentally conscious arts center. The ground floor would house the Tons' idea: 732 Social.

The Tons told food writer Steve Coomes that they were inspired by Avec, an award-winning Chicago restaurant where diners shared tables with strangers in a communal setting. While Steven Ton wasn't sure Louisville was ready for a true communal experience, he said the 732 Social experience would be "like family-style dining, though…sitting near people you probably don't know" in the small, eight-hundred-square-foot space. The Tons brought chef Jayson Lewellyn from Jeff Ruby's to turn out what Steven and Michael called "rustic American food with a touch of refinement" and opened 732 Social in 2009 to resounding acclaim.

732 Social "pulses with a distinctive, transformative energy that feels like the beginning of a new era," wrote *Courier-Journal* critic Marty Rosen. Approving of the recycled barn siding and the "noisy, communal atmosphere that has you…rubbing elbows and ideas with the folks at the next table

Entrance to 732 Social. *Courtesy Dan Dry*/Food & Dining Magazine.

over," Rosen saved most of his effusiveness for the food, "a concise list of small and large plates that lean heavily on French techniques and, to the greatest practical extent, local ingredients." Rosen raved about the house-cured Saucisse de Morteau and bresaola, 732 Social's Brussels sprouts and mussels, reserving special praise for a southern-fried chicken liver resting "on a cylinder of chicken liver flan so airy and subtle that it could be the very disembodiment of organ meat." Rosen enjoyed watching the bartenders "employ medicine droppers and exotic bottles of rare vermouths and bitters as they assemble vintage drinks like the Hanky Panky," a Prohibition-era concoction of gin, sweet vermouth, Fernet-Branca and orange peel. A dish the staff nicknamed "crack potatoes" comprised potato wedges bathed in a sauce of cheese and crumbled bacon under a broiled breadcrumb crust. But the "medicine droppers and exotic bottles" got more and more attention. Specializing in pre-Prohibition cocktails like the Manhattan and Sazerac, 732 Social's bartenders made their own bitters, juiced fresh fruit daily and even hand-chipped ice into the perfect shape and consistency for each drink, techniques other early twenty-first-century Louisville bars didn't offer. The establishment "had a lot to do with the push for a better bar culture in Louisville," Larry Rice, former cocktail program head, told a reporter at a restaurant reunion in 2017. Rice remembered 732 Social as the first bar "doing fresh juice, house-made syrups" and the first to have "classically trained bar staff in Louisville." According to Rice, the Louisville craft bartending community could be separated into people who "either worked [at 732 Social] or were trained by someone who was trained there."

In 2010, Rice announced he was leaving 732 Social to open Silver Dollar. The Tons had also moved on, opening Doc Crow's Restaurant on West Main. Chef Jason Lewellyn took control of 732 Social's operation. But while the chef continued to receive great reviews for his food, behind the scenes, things weren't going so well. As Steve Coomes put it in a September 2011 *Insider Louisville* column, "Social's early demise is mostly a sad tale about a first-time restaurant owner who, either by his fault, others' or a combination of both, didn't get the back end of his business buttoned up as neatly as necessary." Lewellyn filed lawsuits against both the Tons and Holland, neither of which was resolved to his satisfaction. In September 2011, Lewellyn announced that his attorneys had "ordered" him to close 732 Social. The small "green" place that helped bring community and craft cocktails back to Louisville dining was no more.

Absinthe Julep

Larry Rice told the *Courier-Journal* he was "a big fan of what absinthe does with other liquors."

3 ounces rye whiskey
1 ounce absinthe
½ ounce brandy
mint sprigs
1 teaspoon sugar
sprig of lavender
seasonal berries

Pour liquors into a cocktail shaker. Add the sugar and one sprig of mint, crushing the mint into the liquid. Add ice, cover and shake well. Strain into metal cups filled with crushed ice rubbed with the remaining mint sprigs. Garnish with lavender and berries and serve with a straw.

2

Blind Pig

CELEBRATED FOR, THEN STYMIED BY, MEAT

"Start with a smooth, dense ramekin of pork rillettes topped with a thick layer of duck fat; follow that up with a heaping portion of sausage, duck and white bean cassoulet; finish with a dessert of vanilla ice cream fritters and pecan-bacon brittle; and wash it all down with a bacon-infused Manhattan." *New York Times* freelancer Hugh Ryan's road map through Blind Pig's menu marked the meat-centric restaurant's meteoric rise to the top of the Louisville restaurant scene in 2010. El Mundo veterans Joseph Frase and Mike Grider had accepted a challenge from Andy Blieden, owner of the former grocery at 1076 East Washington, to "change the neighborhood" of Butchertown, where piggy odors from the JBS pork plant often wafted by when the wind was right. Frase and Grider completely renovated the old grocery building, fashioning the restaurant's bar from part of the 1930s flood-damaged façade.

Early reviewers raved about the house-cured bacon butty sandwich, the boudin blanc and the bacon-infused Manhattan. Joseph Frase was lauded for smoking sausages in the restaurant's backyard, while Jeremy Johnson received praise for his interesting wine list and innovative cocktail program. The pig-focused place achieved what Blieden, Frase and Grider had hoped for, helping earn Butchertown a place on the America Online (it was still a thing then) "hot new neighborhood" list for 2010. Several critics such as *LEO* writer Robin Garr enlightened Louisville about the "gastropub" concept growing across the United States, explaining

Ad for the Blind Pig. *Courtesy Dan Dry*/Food & Dining Magazine.

it as a place "featuring creative dishes...paired with a well-chosen and attractively priced selection of artisan beers and wines from around the world." Garr expressed special praise for Jeremy Johnson, describing the general manager and sommelier as "one of the more drinks-savvy guys around the local eats scene."

The growing popularity of the "gastropub" and its cocktail selections gave rise to what eventually brought the Blind Pig down. Accessible through stairs at the back of the restaurant, past sausages and such curing in a case, was Meat, the bar that opened sometime in 2011. Much more of a speakeasy than Blind Pig ever pretended to be, Meat offered interesting cocktails created by bar manager Marie Zahn and a rotating "candy bar" featuring treats such as yogurt-covered dried fruit, chocolate-covered raisins, wasabi peas and beef jerky. Meat's owner, Peyton Ray, once a Disney "imagineer," told the *Courier-Journal*'s Dana McMahan that he saw the bar as a "living room for the city." And just like its downstairs neighbor, Meat began attracting almost instant attention. *Drinks International*, a global industry publication, added the speakeasy to its "World's Best 50 Bars" list, flying Marie Zahn to London to accept an award. Unfortunately, the attention came with a price as well as a prize. It seemed Meat had been piggybacking on the Blind Pig's liquor license without the Commonwealth of Kentucky's approval. As the authorities became involved, a dispute began between the two establishments, and things began to go downhill quickly.

In April 2013, Meat closed, and the arguments between the parties came out in the open. Ray accused Frase of inept interference into the regulatory process by Frase's accusation of Meat allowing "underage drinking…sexual activity, rampant drug use and sales and so on," which spurred an investigation into Blind Pig's liquor license. Ray told Eater's Zach Everson that Blind Pig owners cut off power, water and access to the bar. As the state investigation proceeded, things got worse for both Blind Pig and Meat. Kentucky sought to "revoke or suspend" Blind Pig's liquor license, partly for allowing Meat to exist in the first place. Then, in an unexpected twist, Ray bought the building out from under Joseph Frase. Frase did not react well, making comments in online forums "in the heat of the moment, about Mr. Blieden and Mr. Ray" (milder ones included "underhanded" and "screwed") that he later apologized for. New building owner Ray kept promising that Meat would return, shifting his battle with Frase to possible eviction of the Blind Pig after Frase's restaurant settled with the Kentucky Department of Alcoholic Beverage Control for $2,500. Blind Pig claimed Ray's holding company wouldn't accept its rent checks, while Ray insisted they hadn't paid at all.

By October 2013, everybody lost. Blind Pig closed, and a few months later, Frase sued Ray "for inappropriately taking money while managing a bar called Meat." Louisville no longer had a celebrated gastropub, nor a world-recognized speakeasy. Frase and Ray would move on to other projects, but fortunately for Louisville, the sparks they made in Butchertown kindled something longer lasting.

Ivory Bacon

2 rashers thick-cut bacon
1 boudin sausage
muenster cheese
aioli
lettuce
1 pugliese or other crusty roll

Cook bacon until crisp. Cook, grill and split sausage. Split and toast roll. Spread aioli on both sides of roll, add slices of cheese. Layer on bacon and sausage. Garnish with lettuce, slice and serve.

3

Burger Queen

LOCAL INVENTION LEADS TO LASTING ICON

Burger Queen wasn't the first fast-food restaurant. It wasn't even the Louisville area's first franchising concept. (That honor, for the truly uninformed, goes to Colonel Harland Sanders and his Kentucky Fried Chicken.) But Kentucky insight, helped by a spilled milkshake and a nice lunch at Casa Grisanti, created a scrappy competitor to Dairy Queen and Burger King, as well as a spokesperson to rival Santa Claus.

Burger Queen began as a hamburger place in Winter Haven, Florida, operated by Harold and Helen Kite. As popularity grew, the Kites expanded to more locations around Florida, setting up their own franchise system in the baby-boom era of kids, big cars and cheap gas. The Kites were approached by Michael Gannon and his partner, George Clark, who were looking to begin a business in Kentucky. Turned down by McDonald's, Dairy Queen and others, Clark and his partner scraped together $5,000 for the Kites' Burger Queen concept and in return got a small black-and-white photo of a building along with the rights to the name in Kentucky. They opened their Burger Queen in Middletown in 1963, serving burgers, fries, soft drinks and pressure-fried chicken, none of which were unknown in Middletown. What really set the Middletown Burger Queen apart from McDonald's and other fast-food competitors in the bedroom community outside Louisville, however, was an idea Clark introduced that seems common today: a place to sit down.

Clark modeled his restaurant after the Kites' photo but altered the Burger Queen design to suit his own preferences. While McDonald's and other

Susan Bandy as Queenie Bee. *Courtesy Druther's Systems.*

fast-food places served food through what Clark called "a little window," his Burger Queen had a dining area where patrons could stay and enjoy their meals. Clark said he came up with the idea that people might like the opportunity to eat fast food someplace other than their car partly because a child had once spilled a milkshake in his own automobile. Years later, as he prepared to run for mayor of Louisville, Clark told the story of how a McDonald's owner stopped by the Middletown Burger Queen, looked around and commented, "You're confused. This isn't fast food. It's a coffee shop." Whatever the competition thought, by 1970, Burger Queen had expanded to Bardstown, Corbin, Danville, Richmond and other locales. Unlike the bigger national chains, Clark saw opportunities in what he called "shopping center towns," county seats in rural areas that attracted people from smaller communities. Clark's dine-in idea began to appear in other fast-food places, but along with the expansion and imitation came litigation. Dairy Queen accused Burger Queen of trademark infringement, seeking to deny all use of the word *Queen*. They eventually settled for an agreement that allowed Burger Queen to continue exploring what could be done with the "Queen" idea but barred the company from selling any soft-serve ice cream. That settlement led to a lunch at Casa Grisanti, a glass of wine and the birth of Queenie Bee.

Joe Bonura came to Louisville from New Orleans to work in the advertising business. After several years in a local agency handling McDonald's and other accounts, Bonura opened his own ad firm. His client, Burger Queen, needed something to help the company keep up with its larger competitors and their marketing efforts. McDonald's, Burger King, Wendy's and other chains were competing for diners with new concepts such as the Big Mac, the Whopper, Filet-O-Fish, Frosties and more. Burger Queen had introduced new items like the Royal Burger (two all-beef patties, "Burger Queen Special Sauce," lettuce, cheese and an "individually toasted triple decker bun"). But a competitor to the Big Mac wouldn't be enough, Bonura realized. What Burger Queen really needed was something to counter Ronald McDonald. The corporate clown had been invented by a Washington, D.C. McDonald's franchisee in 1963 and, by 1970, had become a national figure. Bonura wanted something beyond Burger Queen's position as "the filling station for people." He took one of his more creative employees to lunch at Casa Grisanti, where Bonura brought up the idea of creating a character for Burger Queen. As they lingered over a glass of wine, Bonura's lunch partner observed that children seemed to like cowboys, suggesting "Queen of the West," a cowgirl. Bonura thought Western style might be limiting, so his companion suggested "Queenie the Dog," which Bonura didn't like, because Burger Queen "was not selling dog food." As he finished his wine, Bonura's "Queenie the D" led to "Queenie the B"—then, finally, triumphantly, to "Queenie Bee." Bonura returned to his agency, had his art people sketch a friendly, stingless bumblebee and presented the concept to Clark. Clark later said he thought the idea "was the corniest thing I ever saw" but grudgingly

Royal Burger ad. *Courtesy Druther's Systems.*

gave Queenie Bee corporate approval. The idea also got a small advertising budget, and Bonura began production.

Fresh from her role in a St. Matthews Elementary School's *Pinocchio*, Joyce Murphy appeared as the first Queenie Bee. Murphy was clad in a claustrophobia-inducing heavy helmet, and the first television commercial featured children recruited from Bonura's neighborhood following Queenie Bee to the catchy tune of "It's Burger Queen for Me," a jingle closely related to the song "An Actor's Life for Me" from the 1940 Disney movie *Pinocchio*. Not long after the commercial began to air, Bonura was in a theater watching a re-release of the movie with his children. As the stanzas beginning with "Hi diddle dee dee, an actor's life for me" began, Bonura's children loudly exclaimed, "That's Queenie Bee's song!—'Let's follow Queenie Bee, it's Burger Queen for me!'" Bonura recalled sitting tensely in the theater thinking, "Oh my God, we're going to get sued! But nobody ever picked it up." Queenie Bee and her not-quite-Disney jingle kept on going.

Her costume redesigned out of foam to be less heavy (but still quite hot), Queenie Bee began making live appearances not only at Burger Queen outlets but also on popular children's shows such as *Presto the Clown* and at local hospitals. Within a few months, Bonura began noticing something. "It was Christmas season, and Santa Claus was on the stage," Bonura said, recalling a visit to St. Joseph's Hospital shortly after the Queenie Bee campaign launched. "Queenie Bee goes into the auditorium, and all the kids start screaming 'Queenie Bee!' They forgot Santa Claus was there!" The following April, Bonura was with Queenie Bee when every high school band saluted her with the "Follow Queenie Bee, It's Burger Queen for Me" tune as the bee's convertible prepared for the Derby Parade. During the parade, says Bonura, "every man, woman and child we passed is screaming 'Queenie Bee! Give me a hamburger!' It kind of scared me what we had done."

As Burger Queen continued to expand, Queenie Bee began to appear about as often as the company logo, a crowned Q containing the words "Burger Queen." Queenie Bee showed up at the Kentucky State Fair, handing out coupons for free hamburgers in exchange for bags of collected litter. She rubbed elbows with rivals Ronald McDonald and Captain Kingfish, offering more free hamburgers for getting an A in class and assuring people that everything at Burger Queen was "bee-licious." The Kentucky-based Burger Queen Enterprises changed its in-house newsletter into The Hive Jive, and even the still-independent, smaller original Florida outlets changed their newsletter name to "The Beeline." Queenie Bee and her archnemesis, John B. Catcher, appeared in puzzles, on Halloween masks and on other freebies. Burger Queen introduced "breakfast on a bun" around the same time the world was introduced to Egg McMuffins. And around Louisville, Queenie Bee kept getting more popular. Joyce Murphy couldn't handle every request for Queenie Bee. That's when Ronald McDonald's daughter stepped in.

Bonura had hired local actor, magician and clown Lou Bandy to play Ronald McDonald when the ad man handled that account, and he reached out to the actor about a backup Queenie Bee. Lou suggested his daughter Susan. As Lou continued appearing as Ronald, Susan began substituting for Murphy, who decided she'd rather return to the stage than spend weekends in a car with a bee suit. Susan Bandy became "the only queen bee in the land," making television appearances reaching Kentucky, Indiana, Tennessee and Virginia. Susan developed an entire backstory for Queenie Bee, telling children her house was a golden hive in the world's biggest tree. Queenie Bee became a celebrity, as recognized as Big Bird, Ronald McDonald and other icons, especially in Louisville. She became animated in television

Queenie Bee with Governor Julian Carroll and Burger Queen executives at the Kentucky State Fair. *Courtesy Druther's Systems.*

commercials, offering rings, balloons and other prizes to children along with burgers and fries. But the pressures on Burger Queen, a small player in the expanding fast-food industry, were something Queenie Bee and her golden hive couldn't solve.

Burger Queen Enterprises put out more ads and jingles touting its fried chicken. They hired actor Abe Vigoda, famous in the mid-1970s for his role as Detective Fish on the sitcom *Barney Miller*, as part of a campaign to advertise the chain's fish. Nothing seemed to help, and the company's growth curve was threatened. Burger Queen decided it needed even more changes. Bonura's agency was replaced by another, and a new "don't let the name fool you" slogan began. Still not enough to stave off competition, Burger Queen Enterprises began to feel the urge to visit bigger cities and explore new avenues—Madison, to be specific. Around 1980, Burger Queen engaged Lippincott & Margulies, a New York consulting firm famous for helping well-known brands like Betty Crocker, General Mills and Champion Spark Plugs. After researching consumer opinion, holding focus groups and winnowing thousands of options through layers of review, Burger Queen Enterprises decided it would adopt a new name that freed it from the burden of "burger." Instead of Burger Queen, there would be Druther's Restaurants. "The change to Druther's is the cornerstone of our positioning for the chain in the 1980s," said Thomas L. Hensley, president of what was still known as Burger Queen Enterprises, adding, "Our new name of Druther's conveys the message that our restaurants have a variety of menu selections to satisfy a wide range of personal preferences." As for Queenie Bee, while saying that she had "the same liabilities" as the restaurant she came from, director of advertising Mark Hughes said that "no final decision" had been made about whether she would stay as the voice of a restaurant she was no longer named for.

Changing the name of an established brand, especially one with a unique and memorable icon, is never an easy task. The crowned Q of Burger Queen morphed into Druther's, the large oval space now reading "restaurant" instead of "Burger Queen." The company tripled its advertising budget, spending at least $5 million along with what was necessary for Chicago's Grey-North Advertising to research, produce and roll out a campaign with the slogan "I'd ruther go to Druther's Restaurant." As the new campaign began, Thomas Hensley was still deciding what to do with Queenie Bee, saying he and his agency partners were surprised that, instead of their new name and advertising, the bee's future was "what everybody wants to know about." Concepts for television commercials had Queenie Bee venturing from her golden hive, telling children she would "ruther be a Druther's bee," but those spots never went on the air.

In early 1982, Bill Lahrmann, then a senior vice-president at Druther's Grey-North ad firm in Chicago, admitted that his agency had been working on a new children's marketing program to go with the Druther's name for over a year. Lahrmann praised the power of Queenie Bee but said "the

Post-Queenie Bee ad for "Dandy Dinner." *Courtesy Druther's Systems.*

company was committed to the Druther's name," and the agency felt that continuing Queenie Bee would be "counter-productive." Instead, America was introduced to Andy Dandytale. Corporate instructions described Andy as "a real person" who somehow "stayed young even though he knows people who lived hundreds of years ago." Andy's supposed attraction was that he had witnessed "everything that has happened in United States history—real and imagined." Andy's jacket was said to be inspired by Revolutionary War uniforms, his overalls akin to Paul Bunyan's ("only a whole lot smaller") and his "sturdy hiking boots" were to help him "keep walking the country, meeting new friends." Andy and his banjo were created by Grey-North to entertain his "favorite people," children, by telling stories, singing songs and declaring that throughout his travels he learned "the best place to have a good time and a great meal is Druther's Restaurant." Despite appearing in person, on boxes and in television commercials, the magical troubadour with his stickered suitcase and string tie who "saw Paul Bunyan eat a tree" did not seem to help Druther's against the fast-food competition. Joe Bonura's agency was asked to return sometime around 1990, and Andy Dandytale was already gone. Bonura was happy that Dandytale wasn't around—had the banjo-strumming focus-group product been standing there, "I would have walked in and shot him in the head."

In 1991, Druther's, the former Burger Queen, became part of its old legal nemesis, Dairy Queen. Druther's owner, Thomas Hensley, declared that Dairy Queen's Blizzards and other soft-serve treats "added a new dimension" to the menu. The marketing research, money and time spent to create an idea by big-city agencies hadn't helped Druther's stand out in the market. There are still plenty of materials left at Druther's Systems, outlining everything Andy Dandytale was supposed to do. How much money was spent developing Andy Dandytale may never be known, but Joe Bonura knows how much it cost to come up with Queenie Bee. "$350," said Bonura. "$350, to get a Ronald McDonald in Louisville."

4

Casa Grisanti

FROM PLASTER FACTORY TO PARADIGM OF LOUISVILLE DINING

The ornamental plaster ceilings and decorations of Pacifico Grisanti add elegance and drama to St. James Catholic Church and the Pendennis Club to this day. But while the Italian artisan from Gromignana created lasting Louisville monuments, his descendants built the family name into something celebrated not only in Louisville but also across America.

Pacifico and his brother Zeffiro Grisanti built their plaster business out of a warren of homes on Fehr Avenue, named for the brewery that had been in operation since shortly after the Civil War. The Great Depression and changing decorative styles led in the 1930s to the formation of the G.M.G Art and Novelty Company, where Pacifico turned out pink flamingos and other plaster novelties with his sons Albert and Ferdinand and their cousin Dorina Mattei. After Pacifico's death in 1955, with a flood of cheaper plastic imports crushing the plaster novelty business, Albert, Ferdinand and Dorina decided that the novelty factory would instead be an Italian restaurant. Dorina Mattei would do the cooking, Albert Grisanti would handle the books and Ferdinand (known as Ferd) Grisanti would be the host. Mattei's cooking had already been noticed by the local media. Cookbook author and *Courier-Journal* food columnist Cissy Gregg wrote about Mattei's "reputation for good food" and cooking "the orthodox way of Lucca," referring to a region in Tuscany, Italy.

From the start, Albert Grisanti dreamed of a place successful enough that it could spawn a line of Grisanti restaurants. Early advertising emphasized "delicately seasoned" northern Italian food, a possible signal to garlic-fearing Louisvillians, along with assurances that their "favorite chicken, steak and seafood" would also be available. Plaster dust swept away, Casa Grisanti boasted of an "unusual" vineyard, murals and a family coat of arms decorating the former factory. The plastic grapes, wood paneling and red plush carpeting in the entrance and dining rooms may not have been that "unusual," but family recipes and friendly service kept bringing people in, and Casa Grisanti continued to grow. In 1964, Albert Grisanti became the first president of the Kentucky Restaurant Association, and Casa Grisanti added La Cantina, an "authentic wine cellar" with a "unique sunken bar" to better enjoy the restaurant's Chianti wines. In 1968, the road known as "Fehr Avenue" since the eponymous brewery began in 1872 was renamed "East Liberty Street." The address change reflected the efforts of Albert's son Michael, who, along with his older brother Don, was beginning to have more influence on the running of the Grisanti restaurant. Dorina Mattei left her cooking duties in 1969, and Ferd Grisanti opted for cash instead of a share of the restaurant in 1971. Albert, who had failing kidneys and required home dialysis two times a week, began to rely more and more on the advice of sons Don and Michael.

From left: Michael Grisanti, Vincenzo Gabriele, Dominic Serratore and Dennis Davis posing below a portrait of Albert Grisanti. *Courtesy* Food & Dining Magazine.

In his sophomore year at St. Louis University, Don Grisanti got a job at Tony's, an Italian restaurant that to this day receives national recognition for its refinement and service. Don saw Tony's as very, very different from his father's restaurant. Where Casa Grisanti had "turquoise concrete block walls, photographic-print wood paneling, and plastic grapes, flowers and palm trees," Tony's had elegance and fine design—a place to dine rather than a place to eat. After his time there as assistant waiter, Don came back to Louisville and began pushing his father to improve Casa's image along the lines of Tony's.

Early in 1972, *Courier-Journal* critic Richard Des Ruisseaux described Casa Grisanti's decoration as "routine American, with paneled walls, some paintings, but no pizazz." His review noted appetizers such as shrimp cocktail and stuffed olives, two kinds of lasagna, plus "spaghetti and mostaccioli in sundry combinations." While Des Ruisseaux found his veal scallopini "unbelievably huge," he also thought diners would need "an insatiable craving for tomato paste to find the dish exhilarating." Later that year, Don convinced Albert to add cannelloni, a more delicate style of pasta, to the Casa Grisanti menu. After its successful introduction, Albert began to encourage Don, by then part owner of Grisanti's, to "try some of his other ideas." Michael, who had been sweeping floors, peeling garlic and stirring sauces at Casa Grisanti since he was in elementary school, agreed with Don that the changes were needed. By November, Don had also introduced green fettuccine with clam sauce along with several other dishes and announced that Casa Grisanti would soon introduce "full French service, meaning more formal wait staff and tableside preparations." In 1973, Casa Grisanti announced a wine school led by Don Grisanti with courses created "by Manhattan's most famous restaurant, The Four Seasons."

Don and Michael made more changes to Casa Grisanti after their father died in January 1974. They removed the plastic grapes and the turquoise walls, began to encourage reservations and barred male customers from entering the main dining room without jackets. But the biggest change to Casa Grisanti from a place with "no pizazz" to something setting new standards for Louisville dining was an idea Don Grisanti had since his time at Tony's—convincing maître d' Vincenzo Gabriele to come to Louisville.

As Gabriele remembers it, Don Grisanti began talking to him about coming to Louisville as early as 1970, when Gabriele was "doing great" at Tony's. When he arrived in 1975, he was shocked to find Casa Grisanti serving only about 40 people per night, far fewer than the 250 he was used

Table set at Casa Grisanti. *Courtesy* Food & Dining Magazine.

to handling at Tony's. After wondering "What the hell did I do?," Gabriele got to work and began improving the service and style of the restaurant. Six months later, Don and Michael Grisanti made Gabriele their partner. As the 1970s ended, Casa Grisanti was very, very different from the restaurant Dorina, Ferd and Al had started. And while many new customers were coming, some of the old customers weren't too happy about the change. Gabriele said "about 95 percent" of Casa's customers had only begun coming since he took over the kitchen, though Michael acknowledged they had managed to "convert" some of the old customers to the lighter, fancier format of the upscale Casa Grisanti. The partners announced a "peace offering" (and new profit center) for former Grisanti customers, featuring "the traditional kind of Italian cooking" they had come to expect. Mamma Grisanti's, located in Dupont Square and compartmented into "ersatz Victorian" bed, dining and kitchen-esque rooms, was described as "not as fancy, not as overwhelming in service and not as subtle in taste" as the "expensive but excellent Casa Grisanti" when it opened in 1976.

As Mamma's created new business and mollified former customers, Grisanti Inc. continued to elevate the standards at its flagship restaurant. The *Mobil Travel Guide* named Casa Grisanti "one of the outstanding restaurants of the world," and local reviewers also applauded. Calling Casa Grisanti "Louisville's sterling example," *Courier-Journal* restaurant critic John Finley wrote that "Casa Grisanti has, quite simply, become unexcelled in the quality of its food and service." Finley delighted over the Dover sole trimmed and deboned at his table, finding the fish "as sweet and succulent as fresh crab or lobster." He also enjoyed other tableside preparations such as trenette al pesto and Caesar salad, though he did add that "all of this table-side attention comes at a price," as tuxedoed waiters seemed "ever to be looming up close at hand; [and] trays of dishes…always to be passing overhead." But cramped as the restaurant may have seemed with its endless tableside service, Finley declared Casa Grisanti to be the standard "by which really good restaurants in this area must be judged."

The success of Casa Grisanti, along with that of its "peace offering" sister restaurant, meant new opportunities for the Grisanti brothers in the 1980s. For Don, that meant leaving the business entirely. Like his uncle Ferd before him, Don sold his share of the Grisanti restaurant business to his brother Michael and partner Gabriele. After studying in New York, Don ended up living in San Francisco, where Michael believed he would take up art collecting after deciding "he'd accomplished all he wanted to in restaurants." Michael, on the other hand, had not nearly accomplished all he wanted to. After thinking about relocating Casa Grisanti to a revitalizing Main Street, in 1981, he and Gabriele announced instead the opening of Sixth Avenue, a restaurant that would seat about twice the number of people Casa Grisanti could and would focus on "American" cuisine. The company brought in more chefs, including Dominic Serratore and Frank Yang, who in 1981 became executive chef overseeing Sixth Avenue, Casa Grisanti and Mamma Grisanti's.

As Gabriele and Grisanti's corporate responsibilities grew, the original Grisanti restaurant continued to earn praise. *Courier-Journal* critic Leslie Ellis noted that Casa had not "loosened its grip on standards of excellence and class that have given it national prominence," the restaurant continuing to provide "pampered indulgence and exquisite food," including tableside-flamed soufflés. In 1983, Grisanti Inc. announced that its Louisville business had doubled in the previous three years and the business was expanding outside the city, opening another Mamma Grisanti's in Bloomington, Indiana. The following year, "to spur expansion," Grisanti Inc.—including

Sixth Avenue and Casa Grisanti—became part of Imasco, the Montreal, Canada corporation controlling the Burger Chef and Hardee's restaurant chains along with drugstore and tobacco interests. Casa Grisanti continued to impress, boosted by a $300,000 renovation. But the absorption into a Canadian corporate behemoth did not come without its own problems.

Imasco kept revising its plans to turn Mamma Grisanti's into a nationwide chain, shifting potential cities and scaling back development. Frustrated by what he termed "irreconcilable differences," Vincenzo Gabriele left in 1985, the company he helped make into a rousing success now changed into something he felt was unrecognizable. Agreeing not to own or operate an "Italian" restaurant for at least five years, Gabriele instead took over management and operations of the Humana Conference Center and opened Vincenzo's, serving "Continental" cuisine. Gabriele's menu included "Eurospa" items such as white wine primavera along with "Continental" ideas such as prosciutto and melon. (Shortly after his noncompete clause ended, Vincenzo dropped the pretense and opened Vincenzo's Italian Restaurant along with his brother Agostino.) Undeterred by Gabriele's departure, Michael Grisanti continued with Imasco, opening Grisanti's Casual Italian restaurants in several cities. By 1987 the Grisanti corporation planned to have thirty-one Grisanti's across America, run

Michael Grisanti in his restaurant. *Courtesy John Nation.*

through Michael Grisanti's concept of "structured entrepreneurship." "I'd rather be lucky than smart," the thirty-five-year-old Grisanti told a reporter in 1987, adding, "I think I'm a lucky guy."

But while Grisanti's luck may have been steady, diners' preferences were shifting—and Casa Grisanti would struggle to keep current. Like Gabriele, chefs Dominic Serratore and Frank Yang had moved on, and even though chef Matthew Antonovich and many others kept Casa Grisanti's reputation intact, the restaurant's style of service began to face some criticism. *Courier-Journal* critic Robin Garr wrote in 1988 that Casa Grisanti "carried the pampering tradition a bit too far," adding that "good service, like good steak can be overdone." Though Garr enjoyed the "lofty, almost cathedral-like entrance…[and] romantically dim, candlelit dining rooms" of Casa Grisanti, he felt that "introductions, tableside cooking and queries about whether everything's OK interrupt you so frequently that…[a meal] becomes impossible to enjoy."

Michael Grisanti cited a "nationwide slump in upscale dining" when Grisanti Inc. closed Sixth Avenue in 1989, though Vincenzo Gabriele attributed its closing at the time to "lack of leadership" from Michael, who was indeed handling several other corporate crises, including the closing of several of the company's Mamma Grisanti's and Casa Lupita restaurants and finalizing his plans to buy back the rest from Imasco, which he achieved in 1989. Grisanti announced that the company would now "rededicate ourselves to the values that made the company successful in the beginning," saying that while some changes might occur at Casa Grisanti, the restaurant would remain "very Italian" and very upscale." But in May 1991, citing again a trend away from "special occasion" dining to more casual meals, Michael Grisanti announced that the restaurant opened by his family in 1959 would close. The Grisanti corporation would instead focus on its chain of Grisanti's Casual Italian restaurants. Grisanti said he had approached people about buying the restaurant but "feared that a buyer might not maintain Casa's tradition of food and service." The decision to close Casa was difficult for Michael Grisanti, who told a *Courier-Journal* reporter that he would "wake up in the middle of the night and hear…guests say, 'It's not the same.'" But others blamed the change on Grisanti himself. Former partner Gabriele said that "one key element was missing [at Casa Grisanti] and that was personal attention," with former general manager Salvatore Rubino noting Grisanti's tendency to manage "from his head rather than his heart." Other employees cited Gabriele's departure as the start of Casa's decline, with former chef Mark Stevens saying that after Gabriele left "Casa just became a void of individual personality."

Casa Grisanti may have closed, but its chefs, servers and other people who made the restaurant a legend began many other standout Louisville restaurants. Vincenzo's, Ditto's Grill, Jack Fry's, Jack's Lounge, Volare, Stevens & Stevens Deli and many, many more restaurants were created by people shaped by their experience at Casa Grisanti. And while the plastic grapes and paneling that replaced the plaster factory may be long gone, the vision of Albert Grisanti is realized—all across America, people associate "Grisanti" with good eating.

Dorina Mattei's Chicken Cacciatore

A few years before Casa Grisanti opened, Miss Mattei taught the *Courier-Journal*'s Cissy Gregg how to cook this Italian classic, also known as hunter's style chicken.

3 chickens, each between 2 and 3 pounds, cut as if for frying
butter
4 cloves garlic, minced
4 stalks celery
2 carrots, diced
2 sprigs parsley
1 large can tomatoes
1 can tomato paste
red pepper flakes
½ cup olive oil
salt and pepper

Preheat oven to 450°. Place chicken in a deep baking or roasting pan and dot with butter. Salt and pepper the chicken, then scatter red pepper flakes. Sprinkle garlic, celery, carrots and parsley over the pieces. Mix tomatoes with tomato paste and pour over the chicken. Pour olive oil evenly over the tomato sauce and chicken.

Place roasting pan in oven for about 1½ hours, turning the pieces several times, until the chicken is tender and brown and sauce is reduced and thickened.

Beef Tips in Wine Sauce

This recipe was part of a large buffet dinner the Grisanti children prepared for a surprise thirtieth-anniversary party for their parents.

5 pounds beef tenderloin tips
1 cup red wine
1 clove garlic, minced
1 teaspoon fresh thyme, finely chopped
freshly ground pepper

Mix together wine, garlic, thyme and ground pepper. Broil or grill beef tips to desired doneness, then allow to rest for a few minutes. Mix any juices into sauce and serve.

5

Club Grotto

KEEPING MUCH MORE THAN A MEMORY ALIVE

Arriving in the middle of the Bardstown Road restaurant revival, Chef Jim McKinney II immediately created a unique impression with Club Grotto. Two dining areas separated by a giant aquarium were strewn with hunting prints, gargoyles, Japanese kites, gilt-framed mirrors, life-sized animals (some clothed) and more. Servers in muticolored waistcoats dished up Oysters Rockefeller, salmon pot stickers, clams arrabiata and mushroom strudel from a menu *Courier-Journal* restaurant critic Susan Reigler said could best be described as "international bistro." Though she thought its decor gave Club Grotto a "slightly sinister, 'Looking Glass' charm," Reigler embraced McKinney's food, especially the southern-fried walleye pike, the Chef's Vegetable Orgy and bacon-wrapped scallops served on crisp corn fritters.

A native of Prestonsburg, Kentucky, and a graduate of Louisville's St. Xavier High School, McKinney started his food career as a Chi-Chi's restaurant waiter, moving up through The Coach House in Lexington before opening his Bardstown Road restaurant in 1993 at age twenty-four. In the early days of Club Grotto, his mother, Juanita, helped out with desserts, but as the restaurant's popularity grew, McKinney hired a pastry chef and assembled a staff, including chefs Michael New and Clay Cundiff. McKinney, remembered as "a man with a sometimes gruff exterior but a warm heart," worked tirelessly to make Club Grotto stand out in Louisville's restaurant community. He made his own mozzarella cheese, plunging his hands into ice water to numb them as he handled boiling-hot curds. As the twenty-first

James McKinney II and some of the Club Grotto staff. *Courtesy John Nation.*

century dawned, Club Grotto continued to receive praise for dishes such as calves' liver Provençale and chocolate soufflé. But in January 2001, Chef McKinney died of a heart attack. Club Grotto closed but reopened after only a short break. It seems that Jim McKinney II had foreseen that fate might cut his life short and had made a request to his parents.

Jim McKinney, the father of the chef, had a background selling heavy-duty trucks, tractors and trailers. He never imagined he'd run a restaurant—and even though she had helped a bit in her son's kitchen, neither had Juanita. Yet, as they told food writer Marty Rosen, "Jim always said that if anything happened to him, we were to keep the restaurant open…so for us there was never a second thought about keeping the restaurant open." Jim managed the accounts and paperwork, while Juanita helped with front-of-house operations. Lucky for them, their son had left Club Grotto a finely tuned machine. Calling her visit a "rewarding pilgrimage," Susan Reigler saluted the McKinneys along with Chefs Cundiff and New, praising their retention of Club Grotto's signature dishes as well as praising new additions such as a salad of baby lettuces with ginger-vanilla vinaigrette.

The McKinneys gave much credit to their staff for maintaining Club Grotto's commitment to fine dining. Other than adding a picture of their son in front of the bar, the couple left the eclectic decor intact, along with most of the menu. The McKinneys and the veterans continued to do things "Jim's way," and Club Grotto became a training ground for a series of talented chefs while turning out southern-fried walleye, veal marsala and other "international bistro" fare for many years. But in 2008, Jim and Juanita McKinney announced Club Grotto would finally close, saying that after so many years of running their late son's restaurant it was "time to retire and get out of this young people's business." Having retired before his son started the restaurant, McKinney could have stayed a retiree after Jim died. Instead, McKinney said, "We weren't ready to let it go after Jim died. It was a part of him, and we enjoyed running it for him." Having said that, and mindful of how young his son was when he died, McKinney added, "in the restaurant business, you never have enough time for family. That's what we plan to do now."

Mushroom Strudel

Responding to a reader request, Chef Michael New shared this popular Club Grotto starter with the *Courier-Journal* in 2005.

For the filling:

2 tablespoons unsalted butter
1 shallot, finely chopped
¼ pound sliced shiitake mushrooms
¼ pound sliced crimini mushrooms
¼ cup dry white wine
½ cup veal demi-glace
2 tablespoons heavy cream
8 ounces softened cream cheese
kosher salt and fresh ground pepper

For the strudel:

12 sheets phyllo dough
8 tablespoons (1 stick) melted butter

Make filling: Melt butter over medium heat in a large skillet. Add chopped shallot and cook until soft and translucent. Add mushrooms, salt and pepper. Cook about 5 to 8 minutes until the mushrooms are tender. In a separate pan over medium heat, reduce wine by half, then add demi-glace and cream. Strain cooked mushroom mixture, adding the liquid to the wine and cream mixture. Reduce until thick enough that a spoon will leave a clear trail when pulled across the sauce. Cool, then add sauce and mushrooms to cream cheese and mix well. Refrigerate for at least 2 hours.

Make strudels: Lay phyllo dough flat on a work surface and cover with a damp cloth. Take a sheet of phyllo and brush with melted butter. Place another on top and brush it with butter as well. Cut the phyllo layers in half lengthwise. Put a tablespoon of filling on each half, then gently roll strudels, folding in the sides to close the ends. Brush with more butter to seal.

To cook: Lay strudels on a greased baking sheet, making sure they do not touch one another. Lightly brush the tops with melted butter. Bake in oven at 450° for 4 to 6 minutes, turning once. If the strudels have not browned, reduce temperature to 300° and bake for a few minutes more.

6

Corbett's

A SIGNATURE SADLY ENDING TOO SOON

"I have had so many people say 'We are so grateful you are here,'" Chef Dean Corbett told a reporter shortly after he opened Corbett's: An American Place in 2008. Commenting on the welcome for his high-end restaurant, he joked, "You would think we opened a church." Within five years, Corbett hoped to earn the first restaurant bearing his name a five-star rating from the *Mobil Travel Guide*. He underlined his point by adding, "I want it. I will get it…or I'll die trying." The converted Von Allmen house in Louisville's eastern suburbs was meant to be the capstone of Stephen Dean Corbett's career. Instead, it quite possibly helped finish it.

It had taken over twenty years for Dean Corbett to reach this point—the wisecracking "Chef Deano" of local media, the chef recognized nationally for his restaurants Equus and Jack's Lounge, the family man dedicated to helping others in the restaurant industry. Born in Portland, Oregon, Corbett taught himself cooking to help carry his mother through a health crisis. After starting his culinary career in Dallas, he moved to Louisville in 1982 to work at Casa Grisanti. Beginning as a broiler cook, Corbett worked his way up to sous-chef at Sixth Avenue before becoming executive chef of the then-floundering St. Matthews restaurant Equus in 1986. He was twenty-three. Corbett's family bought into Equus, and the restaurant began to build a steady clientele with dishes such as Veal Adrienne stuffed with almonds, salami and Danish cheese, and chicken breast stuffed with artichokes, ham, cheese and mushrooms. Local critics awarded Equus four-star reviews, and the restaurant was featured in magazines such as *Food Arts*, *Wine Spectator*

Dean Corbett. *Courtesy Dan Dry/ Food & Dining Magazine.*

and *Southern Living*. As the century turned, Corbett opened Jack's Lounge next door to Equus on Sears Avenue. It was named for his father and business partner, John "Jack" Corbett, who had passed away. Jack's was a success as well, its cocktails (and bartender Joy Perrine) gaining much recognition. Chef Deano became a celebrity on the Louisville scene, hosting the *Secrets of Louisville Chefs* television show, cohosting the *Chef BoyArDean* radio program and uploading instructional videos to his YouTube channel. He was active in local charitable foundations and spent time mentoring and encouraging other chefs.

In 2008, Corbett's: An American Place opened after $3 million went to renovate the Von Allmen Dairy farmhouse in Old Brownsboro Crossing, listed in the National Register of Historic Places. Corbett's redesign blended history and technology. One area of the restaurant promised an interactive dinner for up to eight diners. Linked to Corbett's kitchen through cameras and a flat-screen TV, chefs and diners could speak to one another while meals were prepared, then diners could purchase a digital video disc recording of their experience. All of this was contained within a beautiful building with an old-fashioned wraparound porch, welcoming patrons with white tablecloths, bone china and a wood-burning fireplace. Critics applauded Corbett's handcrafted veal ravioli; a faux "cappuccino" made of foamed root vegetable puree drizzled with truffle, cayenne and olive oil; the chocolate torte with beet ice cream; and other delights. *Esquire* named Corbett's restaurant one of its "Best New Restaurants" in 2008. Critic John Mariani lauded the creamy colors, gauzy fabrics and warm lighting as well as the hot-and-cold foie gras with plums and Southern Comfort gastrique, imploring diners to ignore "the fact that there is a looming Costco about a football field away in the distance." Corbett's: An American Place earned coveted four diamonds from the American Automobile Association and seemed to be on the verge of achieving Corbett's dream of a five-star Mobil rating.

Though he had entrusted most of the kitchen duties to others, Corbett continued to shuttle between Corbett's, Equus and Jack's Lounge and made media and charitable appearances. His burdensome schedule began to take a toll. In 2011, Corbett announced that he was recovering from surgery to remove a cancerous kidney tumor. Though he was told to dial back his schedule, he still managed to stay active, including helping raise over $300,000 for Kosair Children's Hospital at the "Bourbon and Bowtie" fundraiser he founded at his restaurant. Corbett continued to suffer from chronic pain but refused to slow down. In 2012, he relaunched the *ChefBoyArDean* radio show, expanding it to two hours of chef talk. He told an interviewer that same year that he saw Louisville's East End as the city's "biggest opportunity." He began his own produce company to "make a point" about quality control before selling it to Creation Gardens.

In 2017, Corbett announced his four-diamond East End restaurant would change. Taking a page from his St. Matthews location, where his two establishments had merged, Corbett announced that his restaurant would from now on be known as "Jack's at Corbett's" and take a more casual approach to dining. While high-ticket items like Parmesan-crusted halibut and tasting menus remained, the Von Allmen house kitchen would now also offer nachos, chicken wings and burgers. Corbett, now back as chef, said he was responding to customers looking for "more affordable, more accessible" food in a less formal setting. While one side of the dining room still had white tablecloths, the other half was split between the bar, tables of reclaimed wood and a lounge area around the old fireplace. But the shift to casual dining didn't seem to help the restaurant, marooned by the Costco and surrounded by all sorts of fast-casual temptations for East End diners. After ten years, Dean Corbett announced he was closing Corbett's in November 2017. He told food writer Steve Coomes that he was heartbroken, saying he "put everything…[he] had into that place" but was "worn out after 40 years in this business." In May 2018, Corbett sold Equus and Jack's Lounge. Noting the sale, Coomes wrote that he was "glad to see Corbett dial back his workload [as] few, if anyone, in the local restaurant community works harder," adding that "no local restaurateur has raised more money or worked as tirelessly piloting charity fundraisers as Corbett."

But Dean managed to enjoy only a few months of "retirement." In October 2018, at the age of fifty-six, Dean Corbett died of a heart attack. The *Courier-Journal* credited Corbett with "helping spur development in the [Brownsboro Road] area" and described him as "central to Louisville's transformation from a picture of culinary mediocrity to one that's bustling with culinary options and megawatt chefs." The Von Allmen property no longer bears Dean Corbett's name. But through an incredible number of charities, innumerable chefs he inspired and a vast network of friends and fans, Dean Corbett's legacy in Louisville remains almost as strong as when he was still with us.

Parsnip Soup

Soon after his death, the *Courier-Journal* remembered Dean Corbett by reprinting some of his "best recipes," including this parsnip soup with a surprise ingredient.

8 parsnips, peeled and diced
3 tablespoons olive oil
4 or 5 thyme sprigs
2 tablespoons butter
2 onions, diced
3 garlic cloves, minced
2 tablespoons ginger, minced
8 ounces dry white wine
32 ounces chicken stock
8 ounces heavy cream
3 ounces white chocolate, chopped
salt and pepper
parsley, chervil, croutons or crisp bacon for garnish (optional)

Preheat the oven to 400°. Toss parsnips with olive oil, salt and thyme and place on a baking sheet. Roast until browned, about 30 to 45 minutes. Remove and discard thyme. Melt butter in large pot and add the onions, garlic and ginger. Cook over medium heat for 5 minutes, then deglaze pan with white wine. Add roasted parsnips and chicken stock, then bring soup to a boil. Reduce heat and simmer for one hour, stirring often. Puree soup until smooth, then return to the pot and whisk in white chocolate and heavy cream. Season with salt and pepper, garnish if desired and serve immediately.

7

Dobbs' Luau Room

LOUISVILLE'S PREMIER HULA PARTY LINGERS A LITTLE TOO LONG

An "Ex-Louisvillian" introduced his former city to the luau in an 1897 article in the *Courier-Journal*, and he was not impressed. He described the "grossly sensual" hula dance, the eating of poi ("an edible that might pass for bill-poster's paste") and raw fish, and the way a "combustible drink" was needed to listen to Hawaiian songs featuring lyrics that "could not bear the exposure of civilized print." So nineteenth-century Louisvillians and others knew of pineapple, poi, grass skirts and coconuts. But they did not know anything about "Polynesian" food and drink. Though there is some overlap between Hawaiian luaus and Tiki-style restaurants, what most twentieth-century Americans may have thought was native to the South Pacific was largely created by two men: Victor J. "Trader Vic" Bergeron and Earnest Raymond Beaumont Gantt.

Also known as "Don Beach-Comber," Gantt legally changed his name to Donn Beach after he began his chain of idol-bedecked "Don the Beachcomber" restaurants in Los Angeles. Bergeron, meanwhile, accumulated fishing nets, spears and other South Seas bric-a-brac at his Trader Vic's in Oakland, California. Both men claimed to have invented the Mai Tai, and both definitely popularized liquor-laden fruit-juice concoctions and the idea of dining on "Polynesian" dishes such as rumaki (bacon-wrapped chicken livers and water chestnuts) and chicken with coconut and rice. After World War II, both men expanded their restaurants into more cities. The tropical islands became even more trendy as Pacific theater veterans returned, Hawaii prepared for statehood and cultural hits such as the musical *South Pacific* gained notoriety. Louisvillians once again became interested in luaus and leis and were quite ready for "combustible" drinks. Dobbs House, a Memphis restaurant firm that managed the food service at Standiford Field, had already opened luau-themed restaurants in cities such as Dallas and Atlanta by the mid-1950s. When the Louisville airport announced an expansion of Lee Terminal, Dobbs decided that a "Polynesian restaurant, complete with grass huts, a waterfall, and such exotic dishes as po-po and mandarin duck" would be just the thing.

Dobbs House didn't wait for the completed Standiford terminal before bringing the idea of Polynesia to the Bluegrass, however. The company opened its first Luau not in Louisville but in Lexington at the Lafayette Hotel on East Main Street. A reporter noted two eight-foot "tiki gods" standing on the sidewalk outdoors, a miniature volcano and a stalk of ripe bananas hanging by the cashier, declaring that "nothing has been spared to give the place an exotic atmosphere." Meanwhile, in Louisville, amid "the rustling of palm trees," Leilani awaited, offering hula dancing and a Polynesian feast, just not at Standiford Field. Gordon's, a restaurant and cocktail lounge, had been operating on Fourth Street for several years with various themes, including a Torch Room. In 1960, it introduced Louisville to the city's very first "Luau Room." Gordon's filed a lawsuit in 1961, shortly after Dobbs House began serving egg rolls and shrimp puffs at the airport. The operators of Gordon's claimed they spent $40,000 (about $350,000 today according to an inflation calculator) decorating, putting up signs and hiring "a special chef to prepare the exotic Polynesian fare." They wanted to forbid Dobbs House from using the names "Luau" or "Luau Room," but they were unsuccessful. Dobbs House Luau had landed in Louisville, and it would stay longer than the Lee Terminal where it began.

What was it like to dine at the Lee Terminal Luau Room? It began, as an ad headline said in part, with "a funny phone booth." Diners arriving at the terminal were directed to complimentary parking, marked by a pagoda-shaped valet station. They would then stroll into the Luau to "enjoy cocktails—either exotic Polynesian or more conventional…[and] the fabled foods of the South Seas, or the choicest of American beef." While nibbling on "Polynesian tidbits," patrons would be tempted by drinks such as the "Dobbs Luau Bowl," with its floating gardenia and ounces of rum; the flaming "Mauna Loa," with brandy and crème de menthe; and other drinks mixed by Dobbs's "own special beachcomber." A 1970 menu offered "the fabled fish of the Pacific Islands," mahi-mahi, served with lemon butter and chopped macadamia nuts. There was also "Hawaiian Skewered Beef,"

puzzlingly nontropical broiled kebabs of tenderloin tips, mushrooms, onions and bell peppers, as well as a twenty-five-person minimum barbecued suckling pig, which required two weeks' advance notice and arrived at the table with "a lei of carved vegetables around his neck."

The Brady Bunch arrived in Hawaii in the 1970s, and the luau phenomenon seemed to be reaching its peak. But the Lee Terminal Luau Room was still drawing good reviews. *Courier-Journal* critic John Finley in 1979 described it "as one of the better airport restaurants in the country." Finley liked the Luau Soup and his Celestial Chicken, a "boned chicken breast dipped in batter, sprinkled with sesame seeds and browned." (Finley reassured diners that "not all the dishes are Oriental or pseudo-Polynesian, incidentally. Steak and fish dishes also are on the menu.") He also enjoyed the Kona Ice Cream dessert, which he described as "sort of a Polynesian banana split; ice cream on bananas and pineapple, topped with coconut cream and flamed with rum."

As the 1980s arrived, the Luau Room entered its second decade—and the Polynesian aura seemed to fade. In a 1982 ad for "Derby Day Breakfast at the Luau Room," grapefruit was the only tropical-seeming item among a familiar list including country ham, grits and mint juleps. While still offering dinner specials with Luau Soup and Celestial Chicken, the restaurant also advertised "extended Saturday night dinner hours for U of L football fans" featuring steaks, salad and baked potato. In September 1983, Dobbs first announced that the Luau might end lunch service but, in October, instead shut the entire operation down, citing a sharp decline in business. After that, the restaurant and its staff went different ways, with very different results. Renovating what had been Bill Boland's restaurant in Buechel, Luau Room manager John Shanchuk opened John E's, describing it in an ad as basically a steakhouse but with "a couple of surprises on the menu that I've brought with me from the Luau Room." These included rumaki, egg rolls and Celestial Chicken. John E's had a successful twenty-year run, closing in 2013.

LUAU APPETIZERS

POLYNESIAN TIDBITS
A selection of our most popular appetizers, Char Su, Hawaiian Ribs and Shrimp Puffs...... 2.00

RUMAKI
Tender Chicken Livers and Crisp Water Chestnuts wrapped in Hickory Smoked Bacon... 1.85

HAWAIIAN BARBECUED RIBS
Tender little pig Ribs marinated in a secret sauce and barbecued to a turn—an exotic treat 1.95

EGG ROLL
Tissue thin pastry rolled around a delicate core of tender chopped Oriental Vegetables, Ham and Chicken fried to a crisp turn 1.85

CHAR SU
Thin Slices of Barbecued Pork sprinkled with Sesame Seeds 1.85

SHRIMP PUFFS
A blend of finely chopped Shrimp, Almonds, and a seasoning of Herbs wrapped in Bacon, dipped in Batter and fried crisp 1.60

FRIED SHRIMP
Jumbo Shrimp dipped in a tasty Chinese batter and fried to a golden brown 1.85

JUMBO SHRIMP COCKTAIL
Selected Shrimp bathed in our own mouth watering sauce 2.00

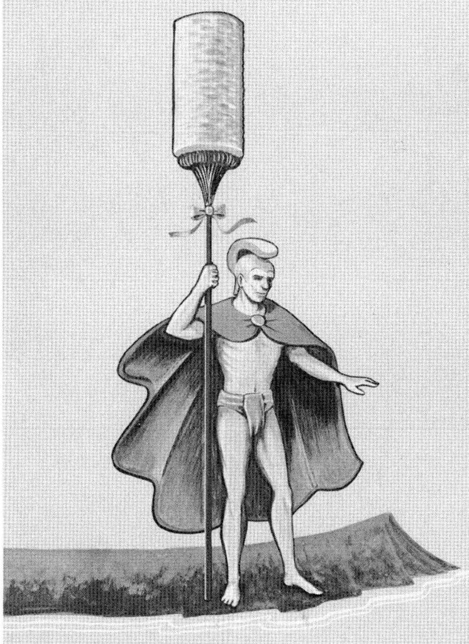

LUAU SOUP AND SALAD

TAHITIAN ONION SOUP
An importation from the French homeland that has gained flavor from its new surroundings .... .75

DOBBS SPECIAL TOSSED SALAD
A heaping plate of crisp Salad Greens, bathed in our enchanting dressing—topped with crunchy Croutons and crumbled Bacon and chopped Egg 1.00

SALAD DRESSINGS

Green Goddess Blue Cheese Honey French
1000 Island Italian

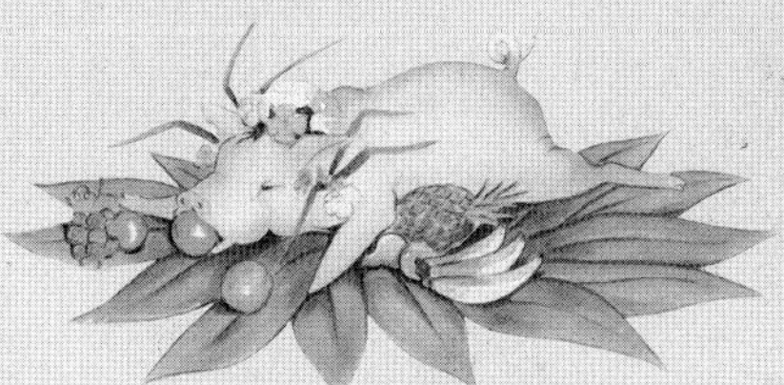

BARBECUED SUCKLING PIG
(25 person minimum — 2 weeks' notice) — The traditional dish for the Hawaiian "Luau" — cooked whole with a smile on his face and an apple in his mouth and a lei of carved vegetables around his neck.

LUAU SPECIALTIES

CHOICE FILET MIGNON
A tender selection from the heart of the meat, marinated before broiling on Charcoal—served with Baked or Bedspring Potatoes and Dinner Salad 6.50

CHOICE SIRLOIN STRIP STEAK
14 ounces of selected aged meat that we serve with pride. Choice of Baked or Bedspring Potatoes and Dinner Salad 7.25

FILET MIGNON AND LOBSTER TAIL COMBINATION
For our Steak and Lobster Lovers—A Filet Mignon char-broiled to your taste and a succulent, juicy lobster tail with drawn butter. This delightful combination is served with a Dinner Salad and your choice of Baked or Bedspring Potatoes 7.00

HAWAIIAN SKEWERED BEEF
Tenderloin Tips with fresh Mushrooms, Onions and Bell Peppers, impaled on Skewers and broiled and served with a Butter Sauce—served with Fried Rice and Dinner Salad 4.50

CHOPPED SIRLOIN STEAK—HAWAIIAN
Choice Chopped Sirloin 10 oz. garnished with grilled Banana and Pineapple — served with choice of Baked or Bedspring Potatoes and Dinner Salad 4.50

Opposite, inset: Luau Room menu cover. *Courtesy Michael Johmann.*

Above: Part of a Luau Room menu. *Courtesy Michael Johmann.*

At the same time Shanchuk was renovating the historic Buechel site that was to become John E's and the Tiki trend was fading like a Grace Jones hairstyle, Louisville businessman Vern Ferguson thought the Luau Room was a good bet. Ferguson owned an old Kroger grocery building on Fourth Street, a few miles south of Gordon's first Louisville Luau. Ferguson obtained the rights to the name "Luau Room" from Dobbs House, along with all of the furnishings from the now-closed Lee Terminal Luau. As the restaurant was about to open in 1985, Ferguson told a *Louisville Skyline* reporter that he felt that the decades-old Luau name "was well known to local people and to travelers as well" and the new location would "maintain the enchantment that made it so popular." He also thought that, while on a section of Fourth the reporter generously described as "ambiguous," the restaurant could attract downtown visitors as well as Churchill Downs attendees. Ferguson replicated the Luau Room menu as best he could, hiring a former chef and promising that the "average prices that were in effect at the time of the Luau Room's closing will remain intact."

Unfortunately, re-creating the Luau wasn't exactly what Louisville had in mind. *Courier-Journal* critic Jack Roby noted in 1985 that while the "palm trees, plastic flowers, ceiling fans, bird cages, fountains, a grass hut and plastic sheets made to look like stained-glass windows" were all there, the decorations couldn't overcome the disappointing dining. As part of his meal, Roby wanted to "find out what the Luau Room does to justify an egg roll for $3.95 when the best local Chinese spots charge $1.25 at most." After waiting almost thirty minutes, he found out: "It's a $1 egg roll with vegetables, chicken and no seafood, and $2.95 for the breading around it. Greasy breading at that." The restaurant tried taking 10 percent off dinners with the proffer of a parimutuel ticket, offering the easy-listening sounds of the Escorts and a "South Sea Islands floor show." In 1987, Robin Garr celebrated the arrival of an Italian chef. Garr's two-and-a-half-star rating called out "the good, the bad and the ugly," naming "excellent Italian dishes" as good but finding the "not-so-exotic South Seas menu" unimpressive and inconsistent. Garr did appreciate the continuation of a Luau Room between-course tradition: Euphrates waferettes. Garr called the Ritz crackers soaked in melted butter and sprinkled with sesame seeds "addictive." After Garr's mediocre review, things didn't get any better for the Luau Room. Ferguson closed the restaurant sometime around 1988. Some decorations may have remained in 1990, when the Fourth Street building advertised "South Seas Bingo, the nicest Bingo Hall in the area," but soon, all that remained of the Luau Room were rumors of grass huts and Tiki torches stored somewhere in a Louisville warehouse.

Some would argue that "Tiki culture" never went away, while others credit the craft cocktail renaissance with reviving an interest in drinks made with exotic fruit juices and multiple rums. Rumaki, teriyaki beef and mahi-mahi are no longer exotic. And some are voicing the opinion that while amusing, "Polynesian" and "Tiki" themes may be problematic cultural appropriation. But no one (outside of a serious vegan) should ever have an issue with Euphrates waferettes.

8

Downstairs at Actors

MAKING THE PLATE, NOT THE PLAY, THE THING

Actors Theatre is celebrated internationally for the Humana Festival and other ideas that keep Louisville culturally relevant. While the stages are for actors, beneath the performances is a restaurant delivering elegant food. The food artists have changed, but the standard was set by the two women who began Downstairs at Actors.

Actors Theatre moved into its current Main Street home in 1972. The redesign incorporated two older buildings, one a National Historic Landmark cited as one of the best examples of Greek Revival architecture in the country. Along with the Pamela Brown Auditorium and the Victor Jory Theatre, the new Actors complex included a subterranean space with exposed brick and narrow hallways leading to some of the old building foundations. Alexander Speer, Actors' administrative director, decided it would be a good space for a restaurant. He asked season subscription holders to submit names, and out of "hundreds of entries" chose Starving Artist for the combination restaurant, bar and performance venue. As his responsibilities grew as Actors continued to gain acclaim, Speer began to search for someone who could take over the direction of the downstairs facility. His choice was the partnership of Luckett Davidson and Gwen Knight.

Davidson and Knight had already been catering Actors' Lunchtime Theatre for a few years but had really gained recognition for the colorful, delectable food served at their Speed Art Museum establishment, Le Café Musée. Both women had backgrounds in art, and they enjoyed elevating simple dishes such as mousse, theirs spiked with Grand Marnier and served with a twisted slice of fresh orange in a white ceramic cup. While they were making things look good in a tiny space at the Café, however, running a restaurant beneath Actors looked to be a real challenge. "It was like going into a dungeon," Davidson said. "The kitchen was preposterous, because it was tiny, ill-equipped, cut up and didn't have any storage." It also had no direct dining room access. "Because the kitchen was separated from the dining space by a public space, servers were always running into people in the hallway who had no idea what was going on," recalled Davidson. "There were a lot of challenges." Before tackling the logistical issues, the pair wanted to make the space as inviting as possible. Gwen Knight brought in a seventeenth-century wooden mantel, lining it with copper and installing it behind the bar. A coffee station was squeezed into a small back passageway, and storage for linens, tableware and other supplies came out of a dusty bank vault through an old iron gate. Old structural work was visible in the ceilings. Spotlighted photos of scenes from plays created a comfortable atmosphere along with tables with white cloths, light peach napkins and small bouquets of fresh flowers.

Knight and Davidson crafted the service at the restaurant they named Downstairs at Actors around the theater. The "opening act" menu included country ham puffs, Bibb salad with marinated black olives, stuffed chicken breast with lemon cream sauce, rice pilaf with apricots and nuts along with a freshly baked croissant. The fixed-priced menu, changing about once a month, was offered for only one seating, beginning two hours before curtain time to make sure people could get to their plays. Dishes such as scallop chowder, cornmeal biscuits with orange butter, Cornish hen with black currant sauce, corn timbale and rice with green onion and ham were rotated in. Dessert options included treats like chocolate raspberry torte or a fresh fruit and custard tart. There was also an after-show "light fare" menu featuring items like potato soup with sour cream and chives or smoked turkey with pickled cucumber and currant sauce on a croissant. Service wasn't always the best, especially during pre-theater rush, when waiters would have to dodge patrons on their way to and from the kitchen (or the liquor closet, which was under the stairs leading down to the lobby).

Jazz acts appeared for after-theater entertainment, and critics called Downstairs at Actors "a convenient and pleasant" place to dine. That atmosphere disappeared, however, when the Humana Festival began. The event celebrating new American plays had begun in 1976 and, by the mid-1980s, was attracting international attention. And all the crowds came to Downstairs at Actors. "It was just wild," says Davidson. "It's hard to

Luckett Davidson with "Captain Kangaroo," Bob Keeshan. *Courtesy Luckett Davidson.*

explain how crowded it was. There were so many plays going on, and we had to gear up to feed twice or three times as many people as we usually did, only faster. And oh yeah—most of these people were from New York, or at least acting like it."

But with the crowds came the celebrities, a little something extra that the employees of Downstairs at Actors could enjoy. "There's always something going on with an acting company, and it was a big company," Davidson remembers. "It's fun now to see some of those people who came through. John Turturro, he's one of the ones I remember best, along with John Spencer from *The West Wing*. A whole lot of now-famous actors came through as really young actors, and it's a fun crowd." Bob Keeshan, better known as Captain Kangaroo, also appeared at a benefit. But Turturro, Spencer and other actors would hold court after hours around the bar at Downstairs at Actors, often until the early hours of the morning.

Downstairs at Actors continued operation into the late 1990s before the restaurant was handed off to a series of operators, all of whom benefited from the experience of Luckett and Gwen—two ladies who took on the challenges of a theater restaurant and made the plates as beautiful as the performances.

Ham Spread

2 ounces Kentucky country ham, ground or chopped fine
1 pound cream cheese
fresh lemon juice
sour cream, optional

Combine country ham with softened cream cheese. Add lemon juice to taste, mix well. To thin, beat in sour cream to desired consistency. Use to fill cocktail-size cream puffs or serve as a spread for crackers.

Grand Marnier Chocolate Mousse

1 pound melted and cooled semisweet chocolate
10 room-temperature eggs, separated into yolks and whites
4 tablespoons Grand Marnier
6 tablespoons cold water
½ pint whipped heavy cream

Beat egg yolks with water and liqueur, then add chocolate and mix well. Beat egg whites in a separate bowl with a pinch of salt until they form stiff peaks. Gently fold whites into chocolate mixture, blending well. Pour into bowl or individual serving cups. Garnish with whipped cream and fresh fruit.

9

Embassy Supper Club

SHIFTING TASTES END A LEGEND OF EXCELLENT SERVICE

In May 2000, almost fifteen years after Sam Pedro's restaurant closed, *Courier-Journal* food writer Richard Des Ruisseaux felt he had to stand up for the man. He thought that Pedro's recently published obituary "fell short" by not providing more detail about his signature achievement, the Embassy Supper Club. Describing the Embassy as "just a notch or two above a cluster of other restaurants in over-all excellence," Des Ruisseaux noted its devotion to service and individual attention, including personalized matchbooks for each diner "except on Derby Eve, when the matches would proclaim Pedro's pick to win the Run for the Roses." He hailed the staff training, with daily quizzes and a "final exam" of 365 questions that "if a trainee flunked, he or she was gone." In today's world of fast-casual, informal dining, the Embassy's idea of an entire evening spent dining, dancing and drinking may seem quaint. But for decades, it was one of Louisville's finest restaurants—on the wide strip of highway known as Shelbyville Road.

America's first "supper club" began in Beverly Hills, California, in 1938, when brothers-in-law opened Lawry's. The menu featured prime rib, mashed potatoes, creamed corn, sweet peas and other Mid-American staples. The idea of a posh, country-club-esque experience open to the general public caught on, especially in the Midwest. And Samuel Joseph Pedro promised to deliver, offering all Louisvillians a place for "those who insist on culinary perfection and superb service." Supper clubs were designed to be an all-night affair with many boozy and beefy options.

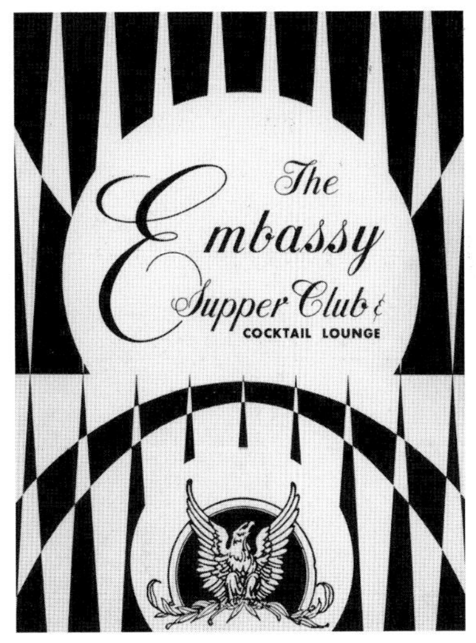

Embassy Supper Club menu cover. *Courtesy Michael Johmann.*

As the Embassy advertised, "you can dine and drink or just drink here." Diners could enjoy and dance to the organ music of Vernon Henritz, while "just drinkers (in the lounge, please)" could enjoy piano music and singing. The Embassy's menu advertised the supper club and cocktail lounge as "the finest dining pleasure for that 'special occasion,'" claiming that at the Embassy, "the Mecca of culinary perfection to Kentuckians and Visitors alike," diners would "enjoy to the utmost the time you spend with us." Oysters Rockefeller, caviar on toast points, "shrimp cocktail supreme" and other appetizers could be followed by pasta (including one with a Grand Marnier sauce) or heftier items such as Chateaubriand, a flambéed sirloin for two, chicken cordon bleu or live Maine lobsters. In addition to Derby Pie, desserts included crème de menthe parfait and Liederkranz cheese with saltine crackers. Louisville diners seemed to love the Embassy and its swanky style for well over a decade.

But in the late 1970s, things began to change. Calling the restaurant "elegant, safe but certainly not exotic," *Courier-Journal* critic Paul Neely credited the Embassy for being "top of the line in the older style of good eating in Louisville." The concept of returning a dime as appreciation for phoning in a reservation was called a "gimmick," and Neely warned that "the ordinary nature of the many dishes offered and the high price tagged on them" meant the Embassy wasn't "the name that crops up when certain circles talk about the better places to eat in Louisville," concluding it was simply "safe food, safe entertainment and a safe evening for anyone who knows the price ahead of time." In 1983, critic Leslie Ellis said a visit to the Embassy Supper Club "left us feeling cheated. We paid those handsome prices for our dinners, yet none was anything special." Ellis credited the excellent service yet bemoaned the lack of spice or seasoning in her selections, writing that "the food lacked a sense of vibrancy and creativity one would expect at these prices."

Despite the growing sense that Louisville's restaurant scene was shifting to the less formal and more exotic, Louisville diners kept coming to the

Embassy until Pedro retired in 1986, closing the restaurant after almost fifty years in the restaurant business. The French-fried scallops, shrimp and frog legs, the cocktail meatballs, the complimentary matchbooks and valet parking came to an end. Most of Shelbyville Road is now crammed with quick-service restaurants. But the site of the former Embassy Supper Club, now a store selling doors and windows, still carries a whisper of its former elegance and style.

10

El Camino

TEX-MEX TASTES TAKE DOWN TRANSCENDENT MEXICAN-WRESTLER-SURF MASHUP

El Camino is destined to become one of Louisville's most polarizing restaurants," *Courier-Journal* critic Marty Rosen wrote in his four-star review shortly after it opened in 2013. "Some diners will object to the sound levels; others will revel in a soundtrack that pivots from Mexican-American border accordion to California punk to twanging surf guitars." While declaring the bar program "superb" and the menu "a magnificent tribute to Mexican cuisine," Rosen feared "some may take issue with the decorative skulls and skeletons" or fail to "delight in watching masked, sequined Mexican wrestlers cavorting on the video monitors." As present-day Louisville has at least three wrestling-themed Mexican places, it wasn't the wrestlers or the music that ended El Camino. It was, as *Courier-Journal* writer Jere Downs put it only a few short years later, "the frustration of too many local palates conditioned to Tex-Mex."

"It'll have a beach hangout vibe…what surfers call shredquarters." That was the vision Sean Cantley, who created the restaurant with his wife, Vanessa, and partner Larry Rice, shared before El Camino even began reconfiguring the former Avalon restaurant space on Bardstown Road. The trio wanted El Camino to be built on three core ideas: a Tiki-style bar program, Mexican food and California surf music. Construction crews gutted and remodeled the existing kitchen, dining area and restroom area; modified the original structures of what were originally three different Bardstown Road buildings; and used existing outdoor space to create an exterior bar, lounge area and open-air seating with fire pits. Opening in the

Outdoor mural at El Camino. *Courtesy Michelle Turner.*

fall of 2013, "El Freaking Camino" was an immediate sensation. Murals and graphics combined Mexican Day of the Dead with Grateful Dead imagery. Television screens shifted from surf videos to Japanese monster films to cartoons. Playlists of beach music and punk guitars blared from the restaurant speakers. An outside patio had its own sheltered bar, and the interior was designed for seeing and being social.

The food and drinks were also celebrated. Marty Rosen called out the craft Navy Grog and other Tiki drinks like the Donga Punch. House-made tortillas and telera rolls held a variety of tacos and tortas. Queso fundido came with Negra Modela-braised mushrooms. Cast-iron skillet "salads" included roasted corn, queso fresco, lime, chilies and chunks of lump crabmeat. For a time, the executive chef of El Camino was Brian Enyart, who had until recently been Chef Rick Bayless's "right hand man" at both Topolobampo and Frontera Grill, helping the Chicago restaurants gain not only the James Beard Award for Best Restaurant but also a Michelin star. Cantley told a local reporter that Enyart had been consulting for El Camino and was "blown away" by what was happening in the Louisville restaurant scene, adding that it was "a testament to something special…going on in Louisville…that we were able to attract" him.

El Camino expanded its hours to offer breakfast, lunch and brunch as well as dinner. The recently-married Enyart, whose wife was still in Chicago working as pastry chef at Topolobampo, said in an interview that he wanted to "have everybody's favorite Mexican things" but also take the encyclopedic knowledge of Mexican cuisine he had gained under Bayless's tutelage and "have a lot of fun with it." Under Enyart's direction, El Camino's reputation continued to grow. *Garden & Gun Magazine* named the restaurant one of the South's best breakfast joints, calling out in particular El Camino's chilaquiles. *Bon Appetit* named El Camino one of its fifty best new restaurants, hailing its "Mexi-SoCal" vibe, its vintage vinyl surf music and the grilled red chile shrimp with red peanut mole. Another mole Enyart put on the restaurant's menu was a recipe that he and Chef Bayless made for a dinner presented to U.S. and Mexican presidents Barack Obama and Felipe Calderón. Seven hours of roasting, grinding and simmering more than twenty-eight separate ingredients made a complex, earthy sauce, elevating a free-range chicken breast with tangy notes of chile peppers, sesame and anise tempered by the sweetness of dates. The cost of this dish was $21, which was a bit pricey compared to the $3 to $4 El Camino charged for a taco—which, despite

Neon sign at El Camino. *Courtesy Michelle Turner.*

local sourcing and house-made tortillas, some people felt was too high. On restaurant comment-sharing site Yelp, one contributor complained "that in no Louisville world should a couple of enchiladas and rice cost me $15."

Enyart returned to Chicago, a town not unfamiliar with upscale Mexican food, and to his wife. Chef Tyler Powell, in charge of the kitchen, attempted to roll with the downward price pressure, reorienting El Camino's menu toward what he called "approachable Mexican." But the pressures of operating a restaurant with shrinking per-ticket table sales proved too much to bear. In June 2016, Sean Cantley announced that the restaurant was closing, saying it was breaking his heart. Cantley said that about a quarter of El Camino's customers expressed preferences for what writer Jere Downs described as "cheap proteins on salty chips" and "beans and rice slathered in cheese, to be washed down with cheap margaritas." That attitude, according to Cantley, wore his staff down. "Mexican food is something that people in this market perceive as cheap," Cantley said, adding that "some people think if they are going to drop money on a meal, they want a white tablecloth and some steak at Jack Fry's."

In 2017, the Cantleys announced that a new, smaller, possibly lower-priced El Camino would appear in Germantown, built on part of the parking lot space of their law firm. That restaurant has yet to appear.

11

Essex House

A WHOLE LOT OF IRISH

Claude, Charles, Thadd, John, Roscoe and Garland Flaherty were born and raised in Rhodelia, Kentucky, along with their six sisters. The brothers began their migration to Louisville in the 1930s. By 1940, all six brothers had converged on Louisville's Brown Hotel, employed as bartenders. They continued to do so throughout World War II and into the 1950s in various combinations, impressing tourists and local bigwigs with their service and skill. It turned out that one of their regular customers knew some television producers and thought the idea of brothers employed in the same occupation for so many years would be interesting to national audiences. The Flahertys first appeared as guests on Herb Shriner's game show *Two for The Money* in 1956.

While the Flahertys were building their bartending expertise in Louisville, Philip "Sap" Essex was building a bakery and restaurant business in Columbus, Ohio. In 1960, he opened the Essex House in Louisville, advertising it as "Kentuckiana's first exclusive pancake restaurant." The combination retail bakery and buffet restaurant featured doughnuts and other bakery items inside an 11,500-square-foot building, the site of the former do-it-yourself store Lumberteria at the intersection of Bardstown Road and the Watterson Expressway. The Essex House of Pancakes could seat over 250 people and promised "25 of the world's most popular pancakes around the clock every day," including Kentucky buckwheat, banana, chocolate and even "Pancake Beef Stroganoff."

Some twenty-four-hour pancake houses remained around Louisville, but it didn't take long for the Essex House to abandon pancakes for a more

The brothers "O'Flaherty." *Courtesy Michael Johmann.*

profitable idea. By early spring 1961, the Essex House had introduced a much beefier menu along with the Shamrock Bar, now home to the '50s-famous Flahertys. In another television appearance on the iconic *What's My Line?*, the sextet stumped the panel, who thought the Flahertys might be farmers or undertakers. Revealing their true profession, host John Daly noted that Roscoe, John and Thad had a "new place, The Essex House," adding that the other brothers were still in the Brown Hotel. (Asked by Arlene Francis what drink was most popular in Louisville, the Flahertys answered "martinis" instead of the expected mint juleps.) Operating the business in conjunction with Sap's, the brothers advertised "delicious drinks, mixed in the magic Flaherty manner," as well as "soft, romantic music [and] a superb dinner chosen from our menu-for-gourmets." Instead of pancakes and doughnuts,

Above: Ad for 732 Social. *Courtesy* Food & Dining Magazine.

Left: Inside the Blind Pig. *Courtesy Dan Dry/*Food & Dining Magazine.

Left: Queenie Bee says "Hello." *Courtesy Druther's Systems.*

Below: Cliff Wisdom, Floyd Williams and Ronnie Colyer, some of the first Middletown Burger Queen staff. *Courtesy Druther's Systems.*

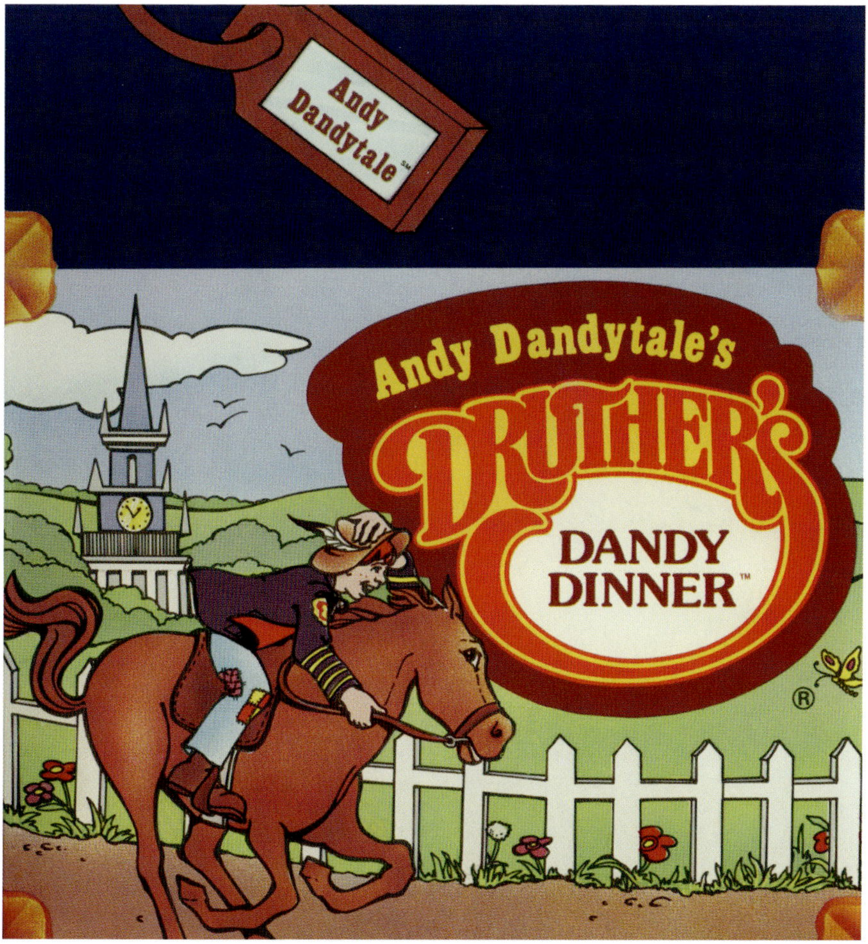

Above: Andy Dandytale's Dandy Dinner Box. *Courtesy Druther's Systems*.

Left: Andy Dandytale. *Courtesy Druther's Systems*.

Above: Outside Bus Parsons's River Creek Inn. *Courtesy John Nation*.

Left: Casa Grisanti desserts. *Courtesy John Nation*.

From left to right: first row: Sharon Risinger, Nancy Russman, Michael Grisanti, Tim Coury, Steve Clements; second row: Manoosh Khosrowshahi, Majid Ghavami, Susan Seiller, Dominic Serratore, Dean Corbett, Mark Stevens, Richard Lewis; third row: Cindy Rubino, Sal Rubino, Debbie Richter-Keller, Kerry Wells, David Cahill, Franklin Yang, Bill Hisle, Kevin Daly. *Courtesy Dan Dry/*Food & Dining Magazine.

Tableside cooking at Casa Grisanti. *Courtesy John Nation.*

Left: Chef James McKinney II of Club Grotto. *Courtesy John Nation*.

Below: Dean Corbett mugging for the camera. *Courtesy John Nation*.

Luau Room menu cover. *Courtesy Michael Johmann.*

Luau Room drinks. *Courtesy Michael Johmann.*

Left: Downstairs at Actors. *Courtesy John Nation*.

Below: Essex House menu cover. *Courtesy Michael Johmann*.

Top: Hillbilly Tea sign. *Courtesy Michelle Turner*.

Bottom: Hilbilly Tea's frog legs. *Courtesy Dan Dry/*Food & Dining Magazine.

A view of Splash and The Islands. *Courtesy John Nation*.

Pool between The Islands and Splash. *Courtesy John Nation*.

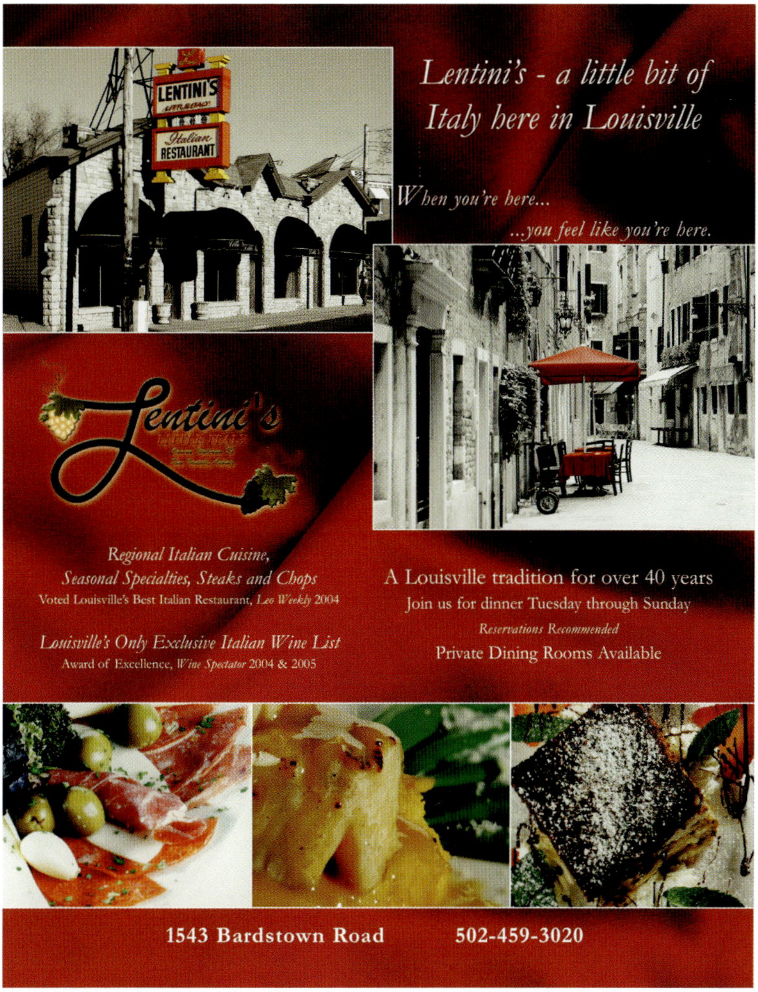

Lentini's - a little bit of
Italy here in Louisville
When you're here...
...you feel like you're here.
LENTINI'S
Italian
RESTAURANT
Lentini's
Regional Italian Cuisine,
Seasonal Specialties, Steaks and Chops
Voted Louisville's Best Italian Restaurant, Leo Weekly 2004
Louisville's Only Exclusive Italian Wine List
Award of Excellence, Wine Spectator 2004 & 2005
A Louisville tradition for over 40 years
Join us for dinner Tuesday through Sunday
Reservations Recommended
Private Dining Rooms Available
1543 Bardstown Road
502-459-3020

Lentini's
LITTLE
ITALY
VENICE
FLORENCE
ROME

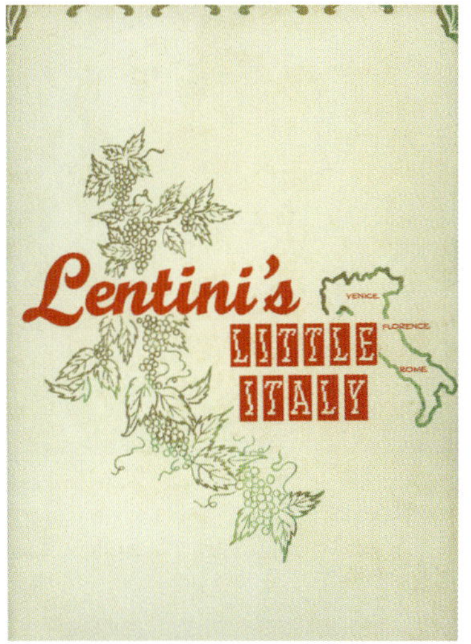

Above: Ad for Lentini's Little Italy. *Courtesy* Food & Dining Magazine.

Left: Lentini's Little Italy menu cover. *Courtesy Michael Johmann*.

Lynn Winter having fun with some children. *Courtesy John Nation.*

Miniature diorama of Lynn's Paradise Cafe created for *American Style* magazine. *Courtesy John Nation.*

Above: Lynn Winter on one of her concrete animals. *Courtesy John Nation*.

Left: Some food and kitsch from Lynn's Paradise Cafe. *Courtesy John Nation*.

THE GARLIC, ROASTED!
THE OLIVE OIL, TUSCAN!
THE POTATOES, SMASHED!

Celebrate Louisville's First Mozzarella Bar

Mozzarella Bar: A sushi style counter serving over 100 fresh vegetables, Italian cheeses, meats and seafood antipasto. Fresh Mozzarella demonstrations on the hour. **L'Enoteca:** A wine library serving fine aristocratic Italian dining by reservation only. **Neapolitan Pizza Counter:** A gathering place with late night pizza & cicchetti mozzarella bar snacks until midnight. **NULU Lounge:** A New York to L.A. style piano bar lounge featuring private dining rooms including a special event center accommodating from 10 - 100 for corporate events, weddings, bar mitzvahs and exclusive parties. **MOZZ 2-GO "Slap Your Face" Italian Delicatessen:** A full-service catering delicatessen for takeout or deliver 7 days a weeks, 11a.m. - Midnight.

Above: Ad for Mozz. *Courtesy* Food & Dining Magazine.

Left: Back of The Normandy Inn menu. *Courtesy Michael Johmann.*

The Pine Room

If you will begin at this end, it will be easier.

Jumbo Shrimp Cocktail 1.95
Marinated Herring in Sour Cream 1.00
Escargots a la Bourguignonne with French [illegible] .... [illegible]
Oysters in Half Shell .... [illegible]85
Hors D'Oeuvres Tray .... (Two) [illegible]
(Four) [illegible].00

Vegetable	Cup	.40	Bowl	.60
Bean	Cup	.40	Bowl	.60
French Onion with croutons	Cup	.50	Bowl	.60
Consomme (hot or cold)	Cup	.40	Bowl	.60
Vichyssoise			Cup	.60

Seeing shall take the heart again.

Tossed Salad Bowl with Chicken and Ham 1.95
Chicken Salad Bowl with Tomato, Egg, and Capers 1.95
Shrimp or Lobster Salad Bowl with Egg and Tomato Wedges 2.95

Left: Pine Room menu. *Courtesy Michael Johmann.*

Below: Ken and Sheila Pyle. *Courtesy John Nation.*

Above: Jim Porter's menu cover. *Courtesy Michael Johmann.*

Right: Dot and Fran's Chick Inn menu cover. *Courtesy Michael Johmann.*

the Flahertys offered fried chicken, baked ham and more at what was now advertised as "Louisville's Most Fashionable Steak House."

In 1962, brother Garland came to the establishment, with Roscoe elevated to president and general manager of the Louisville Essex House corporation. Nephew Gene and sister Anita came to work in the following years, then Charley left the Brown Hotel to join his four brothers in 1966. The Essex House celebrated the reunion by advertising "Say hello to all SEVEN Flahertys. Together again after 5½ long years." A 1968 menu boasted of "the O'Flaherty Clan from County Cork, Ireland…who spread good cheer on the premises of the Essex House." (Claude, the oldest and always only a part-time bartender, continued his work at the Naval Ordnance plant.) The brothers made much of their Irishness, offering specials and long celebrations around St. Patrick's Day. Unfortunately, the "O'Flaherty" reunion only lasted a few months. In May 1968, Garland Flaherty announced a lawsuit against the Essex House. It seemed the youngest brother didn't appreciate the appointment of Roscoe as president and general manager, wanted to see figures from the Columbus parent company and sued. Garland settled with the others for an undisclosed sum, and the "Four Flaherty Brothers" moved forward with their big Essex House celebration, "Christmas in July."

Supposedly begun as a fun thing to do at a North Carolina girls' summer camp, "Christmas in July" for the Flaherty brothers was a multiday celebration. Children and parents were invited to entertainment including a "Queen costume contest for Essex House waitresses," a "host of state beauty queens," a Christmas Parade "traveling 35 miles with a police escort" and a "New Years Eve Adult Party." The restaurant's big stage boasted an array of entertainment, from "rock 'n' roll bands" to "Camilla Wilde and the Mel Owen Four plus Bob Rosenthal and charming Jinny." Jinny, whose full name was Virginia Noakes, had begun playing her piano for the Flahertys shortly after they opened the Shamrock Bar. But a few months after "Christmas in July" 1968, Jinny Noakes, "Darling of the keyboard," would play at the Essex House no more.

In October 1968, in the cocktail lounge alcove adjoining the Essex House dining room, Jinny Noakes was entertaining at her piano bar. Returning to find his seat occupied, John P. Sawyer, Republican candidate for mayor of Louisville, "had words" with Mr. William L. Short, manager of the industrial development department of the Louisville Area Chamber of Commerce. The *Courier-Journal* reported that "accounts differ over who hit whom first, but the accounts agree that Sawyer was struck on the face, and that Sawyer and Short toppled onto a nearby table [while] Mrs. Noakes was knocked to the floor." After working for twenty-one years, six nights a week, four hours a night, Jinny Noakes's career ended, as her attorney said, with "these two men slugging it out, over 400 pounds of man on top of her." A jury awarded Noakes $10,000 the same year Sap's Foods sold its share of the Essex House to the Flahertys.

In 1973, the Flahertys were affected by another fight, this time with plans to widen the Watterson Expressway that would remove the Essex House restaurant, something Roscoe Flaherty opposed. "We feel we have the number one location, with all the traffic there is on Bardstown Road and the expressway," Flaherty told a reporter, though he admitted he needed to keep repainting the building due to exhaust fumes constantly eroding previous work. While city and citizens argued over construction, the Flahertys continued to serve drinks and entertain. Garland, joined by brothers Thadd and Charles, now had a tavern in a small barroom that was part of a bowling alley near the Essex House. Brothers Roscoe and John kept the Essex House going. By 1980, *Courier-Journal* restaurant critic John Finley noted that the establishment's specialty was "fun, not food." The menu put "great emphasis on the fact that the owners are Irish" and that "good Irish fun" included "drinking, dancing and socializing." Describing the steak-centric menu as "expensive bar food," Finley noted that because of the good times and garish lighting, "it would be a tragedy to be served a plate of great food here," reminding prospective diners to order less expensive dishes because "one's palate loses its ability to make any fine distinctions after a very few drinks." At least one longtime customer vehemently disagreed. Kay Hardy from Shepherdsville wrote a letter to the editors rebutting the review: "Roscoe Flaherty, the owner and manager…maintains a high standard of dress and conduct from his customers. The Essex House has a lovely, relaxing dining room and ample space for dancing to the consistently good bands. One can also converse with one's friends, even with the band playing, since the music is easy listening and never obtrusive."

The Watterson, however, continued to intrude. Plans were being finalized to create a larger cloverleaf ramp that would force the Essex House to be torn down. In 1981, a fire caused severe damage to the Essex House, making the expressway issue irrelevant. Roscoe moved the Essex House to the Holiday Manor Center, attempting to re-create what he and his brothers had brought to Louisville for decades. But by 1984, Roscoe's last lounge had closed, been demolished and been replaced by a mini-mall. Garland and various other Flahertys continued to operate taverns about town, but the era of Irish brothers banding together to entertain Louisville had come to an end.

12

Hillbilly Tea

DIGGING A JOKE ALL THE WAY TO CHINA

Karter Louis claims that the idea began on a break as an absurd joke between himself and Arpad Lengyel. The pair worked at Teaism, a Washington, D.C. set of restaurant-teahouses. Weary of doing what Louis described as "very esoteric tea services, full of Asian influence and folklore," Louis said to Lengyel, "We should do hillbilly tea!," only to hear the reply, "What's a hillbilly?" Once the Kentuckian explained the regional reference to the Hungarian, the Louisville Youth Performing Arts graduate, actor, singer and dancer and his chef buddy laughed at the silliness of thinking a teahouse with a hillbilly theme would work. Then the joke got serious when the pair began a journey that would take hillbillies, teas, bento boxes and other combinations not only across Louisville but also as far away as China.

Hillbilly Tea opened on First Street in 2010, offering over a dozen types of tea along with food "from the kettle, creek and pit." The menu may have played off broad stereotypes, using words like "roadkill" and "hooch," but the smoked catfish, biscuits and gravy and chicken-fried tofu with white bean and sage fritters weren't playing around. *Courier-Journal* critic Marty Rosen called Hillbilly Tea "the most imaginative lunch spot in the city," praising it for "the best Southern-style sweet tea this side of paradise," the "luxurious" sorrel and potato soup and a corn vinaigrette, "each yellow kernel crisp, tender and touched by a subtle, smoky hint of Lapsang souchong tea." Rosen thought the best deal of all may have been the Billybox Special, a "rustic wooden bento box" holding items like breaded pork cutlets and roasted

Hillbilly Tea's Karter Louis (*left*) and Arpad Lengyel. *Courtesy Dan Dry*/Food & Dining Magazine.

sweet potatoes or cucumbers in dill-infused sour cream. The backdrop of jazz and classical music quickly grew hard to hear among the crowds.

In the spring of 2011, Hillbilly Tea expanded upstairs and obtained a liquor license. By the summer, Louis was thinking beyond First Street. He talked about expanding the Hillbilly Tea concept along what he called "the Appalachian Ridge," including cities like Pittsburgh, Nashville and Durham, North Carolina. He also imagined other, non-hillbilly concepts such as Galettes, a French patisserie, and Method, "a fine-dining concept." None of these arose in the next year, and the First Street Hillbilly Tea kept infusing vodka and dishing up "pork & pone" (pulled pork on corn pone with garlic mayonnaise), forest mushroom pot pie and "rolled up oysters." In 2013, however, another Hillbilly Tea opened—this one in Shanghai. Louis said he'd been in China working on another concept when he realized the idea might work in that country, where, after all, tea is quite the big deal. Along with clothespin napkin holders and Mason jar mugs of sweet tea, pork and pone came to Asia. The first Hillbilly Tea continued to enjoy popularity, opening a new rooftop patio the same summer its sister opened in Shanghai. The following summer, as Hillbilly Tea continued to enjoy four-star reviews for "rustic chic" items like "hellbelly" frog legs and the Billy

Goat Burger, Louis announced he was opening a smaller version of Hillbilly Tea on Baxter Avenue and making plans for an outpost in Louisville's Portland neighborhood. The Baxter store opened, but Portland never did—in fact, the Hillbilly Tea empire was beginning to unravel. Arpad Lengyel left shortly after the Baxter branch was announced.

"In 2014, we were headed toward a record year," Louis told the *Courier-Journal*. But that fall, construction on the nearby new bridge over the Ohio River isolated Hillbilly Tea's block on First Street. And Louis's attention may have been diverted into thinking of other places for Hillbilly Teas. There was talk of an "Appalachian sushi restaurant" and a "Hillbilly Tea Shack" at Funtown Mountain, the doomed idea to repurpose the abandoned amusement park Guntown Mountain near Cave City. But the construction forced Louis to close the original Hillbilly Tea in May 2015. The Barret Avenue outpost expanded its hours, and Louis still talked of opening a place in Portland. In January 2016, some new partners enabled Louis to relaunch a downtown Hillbilly Tea, this time on Main Street. Some family hardships forced Louis to close the Shanghai outpost of Hillbilly Tea, and he finally said he was through thinking about Portland. "I came here to do a tiny project, a tea shop that exploded into this huge brand, and that wasn't

Hillbilly Tea. *Courtesy Dan Dry/*Food & Dining Magazine.

my intention," Louis told a reporter, adding, "I want to focus more on my creative side. Louisville knows me as a restaurateur but the rest of the world knows me as a singer." By December 2016, Louis had shuttered Hillbilly Tea for the final time.

While Louis continued on with his musical career, some in Louisville, including food writer Steve Coomes, groused about Louis's management, his attention span and his "clearly flawed (and/or poorly executed) concept." Yet the complaints could not take away from the fact that this silly, rather simple joke among some tired restaurant workers turned into an international sensation. And as "Appalachian cuisine" seems to be having some sort of renaissance, perhaps the joke is on those who doubted Karter Louis.

Sorghum Cider Dressing

Karter Louis shared this recipe with *LEO Weekly*'s Remy Sisk in 2016, shortly after Hillbilly Tea opened on Main Street. This dressing was served on an heirloom tomato salad with cucumbers, green beans, goat cheese and mixed lettuce.

1 cup neutral oil
2 cups apple cider vinegar
½ cup brown sugar
1 cup sorghum syrup
½ cup honey
1 teaspoon Dijon mustard
2 teaspoons kosher salt
2 teaspoons ground pepper
1 teaspoon nutmeg
½ teaspoon ground ginger

Combine ingredients in a pot and simmer over medium heat for a few minutes, then raise the temperature to high and whisk rapidly for a minute or so. Remove from heat and let cool.

13

The Hangouts of Harrods Creek

THE PINE ROOM, BUS PARSONS' AND CHICK INN

Harrods Creek was a settlement before Louisville was a city. Flatboat crews stopping before the Falls of the Ohio made Harrods Tavern a popular place as early as 1775. Part of that tavern can be found today inside Captain's Quarters, one of the many bars and restaurants that have for centuries catered to boaters from the banks of Harrods Creek. Through floods, fires and several name and address swaps, three particular places have cemented themselves in the minds of many Louisvillians: the Pine Room, Chick Inn and Bus Parsons's River Creek Inn.

PART ONE: THE PINE ROOM

Around 1932, Julius Ringol bought a two-story grocery on a bend of River Road near Harrods Creek. He turned the grocery part into a bar and began hosting his friends and others at what he named "Ringol's Pine Room." In 1956, William G. Mershon obtained a roadhouse permit, leased the Ringol property and, along with wife Kitty, was soon advertising the "finest of foods" and "generous size cocktails" at their Pine Room. There was also music until the wee hours. One Dixieland jazz band known as the "Fog Bound Five" named themselves after misty late-night drives back from the Pine Room. But the music that Pine Room regulars really seem to remember was the singing and playing of Mabel Curtis.

Curtis, originally from Russell Springs, Kentucky, began piano instruction (using the Vincent Lopez method) and appearing on local radio in the late 1930s. By the 1950s "Mabel Curtis and her Solovox" had appeared all over town, from Lococo's Super Bar downtown to Iroquois Gardens. The Solovox, an early electronic organ, accompanied Mabel to the Pine Room, along with her local fame. The *Belle of Louisville* offered river excursions promising "moonlight singalongs" with Mabel. Described as a "gravel-voiced 'whiskey tenor,'" Mabel sat at the bar and sipped Scotch between songs. People gathered around the piano to sing along as she played "The Whiffenpoof Song" and "Dixie" (when the Confederate anthem played, patrons would stand). By popular demand (and only after she had a few Scotches in her), Mabel would sing off-color versions of songs such as "Roll Me Over in the Clover." Pine Room regulars danced on the marble floor to her music, ate the cooking of Miss Mary Lewis and enjoyed the pleasant breezes near Harrods Creek. Dr. William C. Cheatham, one of the partners who took over after the Mershons retired in the mid-1970s, described Mabel as a woman "who could handle the crowds. People that got drunk and sang loud, she could sing louder than. People who wanted to sing sweetly—she could do that too."

Cheatham and the other new owners promised that people would still find Mabel at the organ. But Curtis, who had suffered a stroke around 1970 and taken a few years to recover, retired soon after a kitchen fire forced the Pine Room to close. The redecoration included a four-foot-by-six-foot oil painting of Mabel, but partner William Faversham knew the Pine Room needed a new musical act. He brought in bands, including the Cumberlands, who Faversham proudly said he helped make "very famous back in the day." Faversham put through several different ideas for the restaurant before his tenure ended, including a series of comedic advertisements and posters. His pine-tree-shaped menu included categories titled "The Beauty of Certainty" and "The Sinful Itch," offering selections spanning country ham sandwiches to flaming Chateaubriand (for two), pepper steak ("for pulsating palate") and grasshopper pie. Things were still hopping at the Pine Room, even though the Mershons had gone. But the party ended in 1977, when the Pine Room kitchen once again caught fire.

The fire department declared the building "totally gutted." The cause of the blaze was never truly determined, though Faversham says some people suspected ulterior motives. "I was in the Butchertown Pub at the time [the Pine Room] burned down. Someone came up to me and said 'you want to know who burned down the Pine Room? He's right over there.' I didn't want

Above: Outside the Pine Room. *Courtesy William Faversham.*

Left: Inside the Pine Room. *Courtesy William Faversham.*

to look." The owners and others initially discussed rebuilding, even seeking zoning adjustments for "the new Pine Room." For the moment, the Pine Room seemed finished, its marble dance floor now just a remnant in a former owner's Cherokee Park home. The former Pine Room location became a real estate office and several other businesses, but the Pine Room memories of Mabel, music and entertainment would not go away. In 2018 a new Pine Room opened, offering fine dining, drinks and musical entertainment. Its neon green sign is where the Chick Inn used to be.

PART TWO: CHICK INN

It is unclear when or how W.L. Bader came up with the endearing name, but by 1943, he was unequivocal that the Chick Inn was "his only means of livelihood" at a zoning hearing, where he also declared that the inn was "not one of those 'juke joints.'" Whatever it was, the Chick Inn was delivering on its name. In 1945, a New York photographer declared Bader's chicken sandwich "the best he ever ate." But as the years passed, the inn broadened its menu along with other Harrods Creek institutions like the Pine Room. A 1970 menu for "Dot and Fran's Chick Inn" includes seafood dinners, breakfast items and a variety of sandwiches in addition to several ways to enjoy chicken parts, from a chicken leg "sandwich" to chicken livers and "golden fried chicken."

The Chick Inn and its chicken continued to attract a wide cross-section of Louisville life. In 1987, then-owner Kathy Dollinger noted that the inn got both "Cadillacs and pickup trucks in the parking lot," adding that one of her regulars "said the Chick Inn is the new yuppie place. I said, 'What in the world is a yuppie?'" The young professionals were joined by the usual assortment of "river rats" and the occasional biker rally. Even into the twenty-first century, national magazines such as *Southern Living* were touting the Chick Inn for its "appetizing homestyle food." But in 2002, like the Pine Room, the Chick Inn was destroyed by fire. When firefighters arrived, smoke and flames were already shooting through the roof from a blaze evidently caused by an electrical problem. The flames became so intense that fire crews were briefly evacuated when the roof threatened to collapse.

Regulars were crestfallen that the Chick Inn's chicken was no more. Saying it had "an atmosphere like nowhere else around the area," regular Damien Prather was spurred by the charred remains of the Chick Inn to recall the small kitchen, the "nice little bar, kind of L-shaped bar" and how the Chick Inn "was just a real family place." Years of history, autographs and photographs were destroyed in moments, but owner Dollinger rebuilt within a year. In 2004, she decided to retire, turning the Chick Inn over to four former customers: Mark and Barbara Mackovic and Don and Sharon Sheer. The three accountants and one public-relations person had no restaurant experience between them but declared that they wanted the Chick Inn to stay "just the way it is." And for several years, the rebuilt Chick Inn did seem to stay the same. *Courier-Journal* critic Mary Rosen wrote in 2008 that he was "utterly confident the Chick Inn's fried chicken

Dot and Fran's Chick Inn.

SANDWICHES

Club	$1.25	Baked Ham	$ .60
Ham and Cheese Club	1.25	Cheeseburger	.45
Bacon and Tomato	70	Hamburger	.40
Ham and Cheese	90	Fillet of Sole	.65
Chicken Breast	75	Cat Fish	.60
Chicken Leg	.60	Cod Fish	.60
Steak (ribeye)	.70		

Dressed 10 extra

DRINKS

FOUNTAIN DRINKS		Tomato Juice	.20
Coca Cola	$.15 & .25	Coffee	15
Cream Soda	15	Tea	15
Orange	15	Milk	15
Sprite	15	Buttermilk	15
		Chocolate Milk	15
		Sanka	15

FRENCH FRIES	$.25
ONION RINGS	.35
SOUP (Home made)	.30
CHILI (Home made)	.55

BREAKFAST

Eggs with Bacon, Ham or Sausage
Hot Toast, Butter and Jelly

$1.25

ALL TAKE OUT ORDERS $ 10 EXTRA

Part of the menu from Dot & Fran's Chick Inn. *Courtesy Michael Johmann.*

is the best I've ever found," its double-dipped salty, peppery buttermilk batter holding "a pent-up energy, a juiciness that explodes in your mouth."

But the tangle of ownership and estates dating back decades brought an end to the Chick Inn in 2010 after property owners demanded a 40 percent increase in rent. The Chick Inn was no more. The space it occupied went through several incarnations then reopened in 2018—as the Pine Room.

PART THREE: RIVER CREEK INN

Everybody knew it as "Bus Parsons' place," but the man legally known as John Parsons had very little to do with the legends surrounding the River Creek Inn. The beginnings of the ramshackle place date to around 1948, when John "Bus" Parsons was still working as a pinboy in bowling alleys before automation. Along River Road, Jess Kincheloe turned a three-bay repair garage into an ice cream parlor. One of the regulars was Rusty, a Cocker Spaniel who would beg dimes then trade them for a cup of ice cream at the dairy counter, a trick he would repeat until, as Kincheloe's son Mark later said, "it was about to run out his ears." After a few years, Kincheloe leased the property to some roadhouse operators. They brought in Parsons, then reaching hall of fame status in Louisville bowling circles, and the River Creek Drive-Inn began to take off. Patrons enjoyed ice-cold beer in longneck bottles, listening to loud music from the plywood-protected outdoor jukebox and cheering an electric bug zapper each time it buzzed with another kill. People could lean on the rails overlooking Harrods Creek and watch the boats go by or enjoy their food on the patio or inside the mustard-colored building. Bus Parsons' offered fried fish, of course, but also chili dogs, barbecue and other casual fare. Critic Robin Garr declared in 1987 the seafood Special Deluxe "enough to feed the Gloucester fleet," with generous portions of white-fish fillet, jack salmon, fried shrimp and crab cake.

Parsons left off operating the River Creek Inn around 1990, leaving the thong- and T-shirt-clad crowds to his son Johnny. In 1997, after floods had damaged the River Creek Inn, then-owner Mark Hugues (sometimes

Bus Parsons' patrons enjoying the outdoors. *Courtesy John Nation.*

Bus Parsons's River Creek Inn. *Courtesy John Nation.*

spelled Hughes) ended the life of a "river rat" named Willard Bellou. Characterized as a "harmless drunk who liked to cadge cigarettes," Bellou had been living down the road from Bus Parsons' in a storefront that had once housed a beauty parlor. He had already been charged with committing burglary at the River Creek Inn trying to steal beer, but on a Wednesday night, he broke into the inn once more. He was shot in the chest, and Hugues was charged with murder. After the shooting, Hugues was evicted, and new owners took over the River Creek Inn, despite his objections about unfair treatment.

Ward Plauche, Colin Harris and some other partners, all with fond memories of Bus Parsons', took over the River Creek Inn in 1998, attempting to repair the flood damage and improve things by building a foundation under a portion of the building that extends over the slope down to Harrods Creek. The environmental group River Fields objected, as did Mark Hugues, who was still disputing his eviction (and his murder charge). Though the renovation was eventually approved, the River Creek Inn remained shuttered for several years, finally reopening in 2000 while remaining bedeviled by the changing neighborhood zoning rules affecting the amount of noise and other things the inn could generate. The owners threw in the towel, and by 2007, the River Creek Inn was replaced by

Cunningham's Creekside, itself a replication of the legendary downtown restaurant lost to Louisville years ago. Parsons passed away in 2017, but his name is still remembered by the Louisville Metro United States Bowling Congress Hall of Fame and perhaps by "river rats" watching boats passing by on Harrods Creek, possibly hearing faint, yipping echoes of a Cocker Spaniel still begging for ice cream.

14

The Islands/Splash

A RIVER SUCCESS EVERYWHERE EXCEPT LOUISVILLE

Louisville and the Ohio River have always had a complicated relationship. The river made Louisville a commercial center, but floods wreaked havoc on the city over and over. In the 1970s, Interstate 64 virtually separated Louisville and the Ohio River. But by the early 1980s, the city began to believe that the downtown riverfront might be good for something besides the *Belle of Louisville* steamboat. Mayor Harvey Sloane appointed a task force to study waterfront development. The commission recommended redesigning the wharf and bringing in food and entertainment options, and in 1987, the newly formed Waterfront Development Corporation asked companies to bid for a floating restaurant franchise at the Fourth Street Wharf. None did. But as the bidding window expired, Cincinnati entrepreneur Dick Schilling expressed an interest in floating his five-hundred-foot-long restaurant and bar down from its existing dock upriver at Newport, Kentucky, and the WDC reopened the bidding. Unsurprisingly, Schilling won. He predicted that The Islands and Splash would take in about $8 million in gross revenues during the first year, with Louisville receiving 2 percent of any revenues over $5 million.

Though they earned an unfortunate national reputation in 1977 after their Beverly Hills Supper Club became the site of one of the nation's deadliest nightclub fires, the Schilling family had continued to create successful Cincinnati-area clubs. One of their biggest successes was The Islands. Described as "glitzy," The Islands boasted a pink-stucco exterior complemented by interior colors of plum, lavender, turquoise and more

Splash neon sign. *Courtesy John Nation.*

pink, decorated with mirrors, large windows, chandeliers and brass railings. Splash, the nightclub, featured more pink along with three bars, a dance floor and windows overlooking the river. Laura Long, Newport's economic development director in 1987, said The Islands was "a catalyst for development of the [Newport] riverfront." As the city across from Cincinnati began to change and grow, Louisville's government and mayor believed that Schilling's magic could work in the Derby City. Not everyone agreed, however. One of the most disagreeable was Mayor Jerry Abramson's friend, developer Al Schneider.

Schneider, for those not familiar with the name, was the builder and owner of the Galt House and Galt House East hotels as well as many other buildings in downtown Louisville through his business, Home Supply Inc. Schneider grew up in Shively, an area in Louisville's South End, as the son of a builder, quitting school after the eighth grade. Schneider's construction career boomed as a civilian contractor during World War II, when he built barracks at Fort Knox and other area military facilities. Proclaiming at one point that "anything over 50 years old is junk," Schnieder often fought with preservationists and ignored criticism by architectural designers regarding his buildings. But one thing he couldn't ignore was The Islands. In court before Jefferson Circuit Court Judge Laurence Higgins in 1987, Schneider testified that the pink barges would be "such an eyesore" that he would be unable to lease the riverfront apartments he was constructing adjacent to the Galt House. Schneider also swore that The Islands "would attract prostitutes, which he feared would hurt his hotel business, especially religious conventions." Schneider was so upset about The Islands that he broke off relations with Mayor Jerry Abramson (whom he had lunched with weekly for years), fired his advertising agency and attributed a heart attack to his anger. Despite Schneider's objections, The Islands was cleared to leave Newport and come to Louisville. Passing through the Markland Locks near Carrolton, Kentucky, one side of the pink façade was crushed, requiring drywall repair as soon as it reached Louisville.

Reactions were mixed when The Islands and Splash finally opened in December 1987. *Courier-Journal* columnist Bob Hill declared that the complex looked "like sin while its promoters are preaching salvation," adding that "it would easily win—and here goes 10 years worth of Al Schneider jokes—an ugly contest with the Galt House." Schneider himself said that it looked "worse than…[he] thought it was going to," but early customers such as Fay Minyard thought it was attractive. Early on, the barge was certainly popular. Food critic Robin Garr noted in January 1988 that "reservations are mandatory, and reservation times aren't likely to be met," saying that he waited thirty minutes for a table on a weeknight, a delay The Islands staff told him was shorter than that experienced by many other diners. Though he enjoyed the food prepared by Chef Gary Flynn, Garr was disappointed by the "conservative steak-and-potatoes" menu with a few items adding "a very tame hint of the exotic." One of these was something called Chicken Polynesian, which, according to Garr, was poultry marinated in sherry, served in a pineapple and "topped with a boozy coconut-cherry sauce." Giving The Islands a two-and-a-half-star rating, Garr disliked the "crowded, hellishly noisy" dining room and predicted that "unless major changes happen, I suspect Louisville's infatuation with the pink barge will diminish when its glittery novelty fades." He wasn't wrong.

In February 1988, The Islands was cited for launching fireworks into the Ohio near a towboat pushing barges of flammable and hazardous materials, forcing the restaurant to call off the shows. June of that same year saw a mayfly invasion, forcing the restaurant to cancel outdoor lunch service and move patrons indoors, where "a lacework pattern of mayflies covered two windows, obscuring the George Rogers Clark bridge." In December, Chef Gary Flynn departed, with Robin Garr reporting that Schilling, who was already attempting to sell The Islands, wasn't planning to replace him.

In June 1990, Richard Schilling Jr. announced that The Islands would begin operating as a banquet facility, with small parties only accepted for holidays such as Thanksgiving. In December of that year, heavy rains came, and the Ohio River rose, making The Islands and Splash inaccessible for nearly two weeks. In April 1991, Schilling strongly hinted it might be time for The Islands to move on. While in 1988 sales exceeded expectations to a total of $5.7 million, 1989 revenues dropped to $3.3 million, receding to only $2.4 million in 1990. Schilling noted that the flooding, which forced the complex to shut down during much of April and December, was a real issue. In August 1991, Schilling announced that The Islands and Splash would leave Louisville for Tunica, Mississippi, where Splash would "become a dining hall, while The Islands would remain primarily a dining establishment." Rejecting claims that the barges' pinkness was "problematic from the inception," Schilling said the color would remain as The Islands and Splash found a new home in Tunica. He thought that, with a muddy river, "they need to be bright. You need that tropical feeling."

Louisvillians may have felt that their aesthetics had finally achieved a victory as the pink barges sailed south. But the Schillings perhaps had the last laugh. They "came [to Tunica] in an old black Lincoln with everything they had piled in the back and left millionaires," said Brooks Taylor, publisher, editor and the main reporter of the weekly *Tunica Times*. Instead of a dining hall, Splash became DeSoto County, Mississippi's first gambling boat. State law called for gambling vessels to float on the Mississippi River or its navigable tributaries. The Schillings' insight was interpreting "the river" to mean the floodplain of the Mississippi. Perhaps remembering the Ohio floods, the Schillings had trenches dug, floating The Islands and Splash inland to man-made ponds. Surrounded by dry land, the floors of the barges legally became "gambling boats." Richard Schilling Jr. is now venerated in the Tunica area as the "Father of Mississippi Gaming," with many crediting his work building what is now a $3 billion industry. Today, several landlocked "gambling boats" are an easy drive from Louisville, the Galt Houses are presumably prostitute-free and the city's riverfront has had a true renaissance. But while Newport and Tunica might remember the Schillings fondly, when remembering Splash and The Islands, most Louisvillians might reach for the Pepto-Bismol.

15

Jim Porter's

A GIANT BECOMES A GOOD-TIME EMPORIUM

Much like the establishments named after him, the real Jim Porter began small then grew to outsized proportions. Born sometime around 1810, as a young man James D. Porter was small enough to be hired as a jockey. As a teenager he grew so quickly that his Shippingport neighbors began stopping by once a week to measure his height, which ended up somewhere around seven feet, nine inches. Porter became an international sensation, visited by Charles Dickens and briefly "with a company of dwarfs, [making] a financially successful tour of the Eastern states" as Gulliver of *Gulliver's Travels*. Besieged both by gawkers and lingering health problems, Porter withdrew from public life, opening taverns first in Shippingport and then in Portland, where traders from Cincinnati would meet planters from New Orleans to drink and gamble. The "Kentucky Giant" died in 1859, noted as "the soul of honor and honesty" who "wielded considerable influence among his neighbors and friends." Jim Porter continued to grow as a mythical figure after his death, his giant shoe and other ephemera preserved for posterity. Almost a century later, Porter's tavern reappeared, thanks to the Sheraton hotel chain and some enthusiastic mythologizing.

In 1956, Sheraton announced that the Seelbach Hotel was "now flying the Sheraton banner" and would henceforth be known as the "Sheraton-Seelbach," promising "new facilities and new luxuries." Louisvillians, as they are wont to do, continued to call the hotel the Seelbach. But they did warm to the new facilities, one of which was Jim Porter's Tavern. The *Courier-Journal*'s Cissy Gregg reported on the opening of what was being called an "authentic

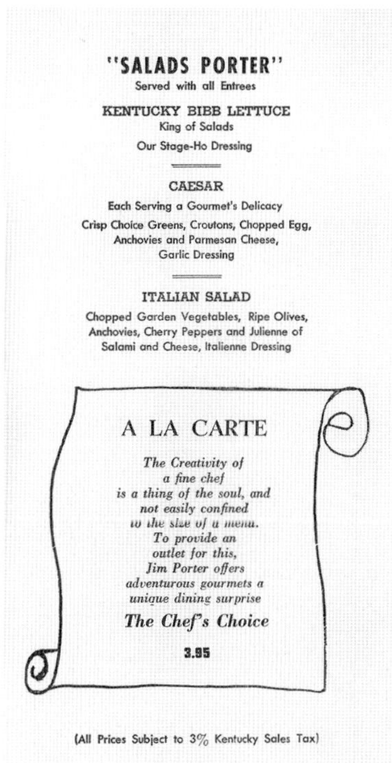

"SALADS PORTER"
Served with all Entrees

KENTUCKY BIBB LETTUCE
King of Salads
Our Stage-Ho Dressing

CAESAR
Each Serving a Gourmet's Delicacy
Crisp Choice Greens, Croutons, Chopped Egg, Anchovies and Parmesan Cheese, Garlic Dressing

ITALIAN SALAD
Chopped Garden Vegetables, Ripe Olives, Anchovies, Cherry Peppers and Julienne of Salami and Cheese, Italienne Dressing

A LA CARTE

The Creativity of a fine chef is a thing of the soul, and not easily confined to the size of a menu. To provide an outlet for this, Jim Porter offers adventurous gourmets a unique dining surprise

The Chef's Choice

3.95

(All Prices Subject to 3% Kentucky Sales Tax)

Part of Jim Porter's menu. *Courtesy Michael Johmann.*

reproduction," saying the ahistorical bar dining room with its giant photographic mural of Main Street was "a joy to see." Gregg related some of the "Rules of the Tavern," purportedly Porter's, which included no gambling, "no cockfighting within hearing distance" and "no gamboling in the bedrooms." Gregg also noted another rule that Porter probably didn't consider: "No ladies allowed until 3:13 post meditation." The Sheraton managers admitted to Gregg that the rule was theirs, not Porter's, "because there's a stock market ticker in the tavern—and you know how men get about those things!" However, during the holiday season, Jim Porter's graciously notified "all gentlewomen" that they would be welcome at any time for drinks and dining along with "Gregor and his haunting violin."

Diners were invited to enjoy "Jim Porter size" martinis, bourbon highballs or Manhattans along with their "Jim Porter cut" prime rib. There were also "salads Porter" along with fried shrimp, sirloin steaks "especially cut for milady," country ham, pork chops and more. The menu told the tale of Porter, "a living legend in action," and featured an illustration of a tall man in what looked like frontier garb holding a large gun. (It is unclear whether or not Jim Porter actually owned an eight-foot rifle.) The Sheraton's version of Porter's tavern was quite popular, its salad dressing earning a place in a Diner's Club cookbook in 1959. In those pre–Bourbon Trail days, the tavern also boasted that it had "America's largest collection of Kentucky Bourbon whiskies." But as the downtown core began to empty out in the 1960s, Jim Porter's, along with the Seelbach, began to search for other ways to increase business. A "dinner theater" promised performances in the Rathskeller with dinner at Porter's, featuring the "5¢ Mug-O-Beer" and "all the salad you can mix."

In 1969, Sheraton sold the hotel to the Gotham Hotels chain, which (as most Louisvillians had been doing all along) renamed it the Seelbach. In 1971, new owner Ben "Sonny" Rogers added nightly dance entertainment and breakfast to "Portersize" the options. Continuing the tradition of inventing things like "tavern rules" for Porter, the management claimed to have "found among the legendary Jim Porter's personal papers…Stonewall Jackson's recipe for the world's best Bar-b-Cue ribs." In 1975, the Seelbach closed, and plans began for renovation. Two years later, Mayor Harvey Sloane announced the go-ahead for redesigning the Seelbach. The Blue Boar cafeteria would become a ballroom, while the Jim Porter tavern would be torn down to provide space for a driveway.

Rogers moved the Walnut Street restaurant to a new home on Lexington Road. Over the next several years, "Jim Porter's Tavern and Steak House" received tepid reviews for its food but increasing crowds for its music. In the late 1980s, Rogers saw what was happening. He renovated, expanded and reopened Jim Porter's Tavern as Jim Porter's Good Time Emporium. Instead of a full-service restaurant, there was a limited menu but lots of bars and dance floors catering to middle-aged men and women seeking entertainment. The "Kentucky Giant" had been removed in all but name. Which, given that he reportedly "shunned rather than sought the public gaze," would probably have been just fine with Jim.

Jim Porter's Tavern Dressing

This recipe was included in *The Diners' Club Cookbook* in 1959 by Myra Waldo, who the *Courier-Journal*'s Cissy Gregg described as "a most capable cookbook author."

¼ cup sugar
1 teaspoon dry mustard
2 teaspoons salt
½ cup cider vinegar
⅓ cup water
1 cup olive oil
1 clove minced garlic
1 tablespoon poppy seeds
1 tablespoon celery seeds

Dissolve the sugar, mustard and salt in vinegar in a jar. Add water and oil and shake until well blended. Add remaining seasonings. Shake well once more before serving on vegetables or green salads.

16

Kienle's

STRICTLY—VERY STRICTLY—A GERMAN EXPERIENCE

Mature woman, must be neat and must speak German." Those were the kitchen help requirements listed in a classified ad for work at Kienle's restaurant. They were only some of the rules Marlen Kienle insisted on. And those rules kept bringing Louisville diners back to the Shelbyville Road Plaza for twenty years.

Kienle arrived in Louisville from Germany in the 1950s, opening her restaurant with husband Adi in 1971. Described as "a perfectly groomed, striking woman with blue eyes and a broad smile," Kienle was an amateur gourmet cook specializing in German and French cuisine, while Adi had worked as the director of a boarding school for athletes in West Germany. To their amazement, the restaurant was quickly successful. Kienle told a *Louisville Times* reporter that "when we started, [Adi] could not fry an egg." As the customers piled in, Adi would stick his head out of the door to whisper, "What do I do now?" as Marlen was trying to figure out how to work the cash register. They managed to figure things out, and the reviewers were impressed. One, Richard Des Ruisseaux, swooned over Kienle's stuffed breast of veal, calling it "a massive, luscious slab of meat…tender enough to cut with a dull tongue." Sauerbraten, Wiener schnitzel, beef rouladen and veal cordon bleu were also enthusiastically received. The quality of the food was due to Marlen Kienle's control over every aspect of her restaurant, something that very much extended into the dining room.

Unlike a legendary fast-food chain slogan, "at Kienle's, you have it *their* way" said one reviewer. He detailed how Kienle, hovering around her guests like an aristocrat, banned blue jeans. And menus. And salt and pepper shakers. And children under twelve. Kienle had perfectly good reasons for her rules. She barred children under twelve "because they might make too much noise." Salt and pepper shakers? People "would ruin their dishes when they are already perfectly seasoned!" Required coat and tie and no blue jeans? "Even though we're a small place in a shopping center, I like to have a nice atmosphere....I wouldn't serve the President of the United States if he came here in blue jeans." But along with the rules, there was the food. Even in the artificial ingredient-saturated 1970s, Kienle refused to use anything artificial. Fresh roses were handed to every lady. She used distilled water for soups and stews, unsalted butter, even making ice cubes from distilled spring water. In the daytime, Kienle's served up Westphalian hams, prepared salads, cheese and other European delights from the deli counter. But at night, white tablecloths and fresh roses came out for the eight or so tables, along with linen napkins and Kienle, who (despite the rules) made every effort to make diners feel "as though you're a guest in her home."

Kienle's kept serving strictly wonderful German food through the late 1980s, even though Adi and Marlen went their separate ways. He opened

Roses of the kind found on every table at Kienle's. *Courtesy Michelle Turner.*

Kienle's Old Heidelberg on Watterson Trail, offering "similar German goodies with a bit less elegance for about half the price," as writer Robin Garr put it. Adi's place lasted only a few years, while Marlen kept up her standards and kept bringing in customers. Unfortunately, the owners of Shelbyville Road Plaza had other ideas.

In 1992, Marlen Kienle announced that she would shut the doors of her restaurant. She said she couldn't agree to the terms of her new lease in the recently renovated shopping center. Her award-winning restaurant was required, among other provisions, to stay open seven days a week and take down the curtains from her windows and her front awning, which caused her German chocolates to melt from the heat. "It's very hard," she told a *Courier-Journal* reporter, with tears collecting in her eyes. "It's quite an emotional thing for me." However, after twenty-one years running a restaurant, Kienle said she was looking forward to traveling, showing her Arabian horses "and having a cultural life again." Kienle claimed she was working on a cookbook of German recipes, but no record has been found of its publication. Marlen Kienle passed away only a few years later. Where her restaurant was is now the part of the St. Matthews branch of the U.S. Postal Service—where there are definitely rules, but unless it's a special delivery, no *Sacher torte*.

17

Lentini's Little Italy

DOWN-TO-EARTH, UNFAZED BY WIND AND FIRE

A bottle of Chianti. An antipasto tray of olives, cheese and assorted salami. Spaghetti with meatballs. Spumoni ice cream. For over four decades, Lentini's Little Italy provided Louisville with a template of Italian dining—accessible and served in big portions along with a heaping helping of kitsch.

Gasper "Sonny" Lentini began thinking of running his own restaurant as a teenager, when he left Louisville to help some California relatives with their own Italian place. Returning to Louisville after a stint in the army, Lentini managed a Mario's Pizza before taking over the bankrupt Highland Italian Restaurant on Bardstown Road in 1962. In an early menu, Sonny Lentini told diners that if they felt they were "in the heart of Italy while dining at Lentini's, it's because we planned it that way." He detailed how "thousands of dollars worth of decorations [were] imported directly from Italy," including statues of Roman gods and an olive tree standing at the rear of the main dining area. Walls were covered in hand-painted murals and prominently featured an 1896 painting based on Edwin Landseer's *The Maid and the Magpie* by "Zimgonia, when he was a student of the great master." There was also a twelve-foot mantel, passed from Lentini to Lentini for over a century.

Lentini declared that the quality of food and service were "duplicated only on the Italian Riviera." While Lentini's menu may have lacked pesto, focaccia and other Genovese specialties known on the actual Italian Riviera, Louisville's "Little Italy" did have a Hot Brown, a dish very likely little known in Genoa. (Asti Spumanti was offered in both locations.) Through the 1960s and early 1970s, Lentini's built a steady business. Patrons enjoyed steaks, seafood and Italian specialties such as "eggplant a la parmagiana" beneath the murals, chandeliers and the Zimgonia painting, which by 1969 had supposedly become "a tourist attraction for prominent art lovers from all over the country."

On April 3, 1974, several tornadoes ripped through Kentucky and Indiana, killing 117 people and causing millions of dollars in damages. Before flattening the trees of Cherokee Park, one of the twisters tore by Lentini's, smashing in the front of the limestone-faced building. The Lentinis took the tornado in stride, rebuilding and reopening a few months later after remodeling much of the restaurant. Advertising that "the tornado's gone, but we're still here," Lentini's still claimed a "beautifully authentic setting that transports you to the heart of Italy." It wouldn't be the last time Lentini's quickly bounced back from disaster. A fire in May 1978 caused extensive damage, but by February 1979, *Courier-Journal* critic Paul Neely was reporting a "shine of newness" on bright red drapes and flowery wallpaper that had replaced the murals. Neely homed in on Lentini's appeal to Louisville, calling it "a kind of neighborhood place that can satisfy, at least for a regular evening out. It doesn't deliver much more, but it doesn't promise it either." In 1989, an overheated clothes dryer caused another fire, leading to another interior remodeling. That autumn, critic Robin Garr noted that despite the tornado and fires, the century-old mantelpiece and Zimgonia painting were still there.

Even at the start of the 1990s, Lentini's menu still noted *The Maid and the Magpie* as a tourist attraction and stated that its food was "duplicated on the Italian Riviera and excelled nowhere," though Garr found he "wouldn't go that far." By the late 1990s, Lentini's was being celebrated as a Louisville institution, with critic Susan Reigler proudly noting in 1997 that "you step back in time a bit when you enter Lentini's. No yuppified dining trends have intruded."

But as the century changed, so did Lentini's. In 2001, Sonny Lentini sold his business to Phat Thanh Le, who split the space into two restaurants, Lentini's and the "strictly Asian" Cafe Mimosa. In 2003, Phat Thanh Le told a reporter that while Lentini's tended to draw "an older crowd," he hoped the Vietnamese and other Asian food might "bring in a younger generation, too." Apparently it did not, as in November of that year, Lentini's was purchased by Kerry Wells and Jeff Grubb, who advertised themselves as "Due Fratelli Oobatz," their Italian-by-way-of-*The Sopranos* phrase for "two

Insalatas

MR. LENTINI'S ITALIAN
(Oil-Vinegar-Salt-Pepper) .... .50

LENTINI'S
(Chopped Olives-Ham-Salami-Cheese) 1.95

COMBINATION

Pure Roquefort	.75	1000 Isle	.50
French	.50	Anchovies	.75

Antipastos

Antipasto, small.....45 Lentini for 2....1.40 for 4....2.65

Sedani et Olive (Celery and Olives)	.65
Pepperoncini (Italian Green Peppers)	.55
Salami (Italian Sausage)	.75
Shrimp Cocktail	1.50
Tomato Juice	.20 and .35
Minestrone and Chicken Soup	.35 and .50

Lentini's Italian Entrees

PASTA CON POLPETTE (Spaghetti with Meat Balls)	3.15
MOSTACCIOLI CON POLPETTE (Spaghetti Shaped Like a Noodle Served with Meat Balls)	3.30
PASTA OR MOSTACCIOLI WITH ITALIAN SAUSAGE This Sausage is home-made and seasoned Sicilian style in a delicious tomato sauce, delicately spiced	3.65
PASTA WITH CLAM SAUCE	3.65
RAVIUOLI CON POLPETTE (Ravioli with Meat Balls)	3.45
RAVIUOLI OR PASTA CON FEGATINI (Ravioli or Spaghetti with Chicken Livers)	3.90
RAVIUOLI CON PASTA MEZZO-MEZZO (Ravioli and Pasta Half-Half)	3.45
CHICKEN CACCIATORA (Chicken fried in a blended wine, flavored with tomatoes, seasoned with olive oil and parsley)	4.25
CHICKEN A LA TETRAZZINI (Sliced Chicken, Spaghetti, Mushrooms, Cheese, baked in delicious Cream Sauce in Casserole)	4.25
CHICKEN VESUVIO (Disjointed Spring Chicken (half), sauteed in olive oil, oregano, garlic and wine)	4.50
CANNELLONI (Special macaroni stuffed with our combination of meats, cheese and baked in a special Meat or Cream Cheese Sauce)	4.50
MANICOTTI (Cheese stuffed macaroni, baked in casserole with rich tomato Meat Sauce)	4.25
LASAGNA (Sheets of macaroni, fixed in layers, stuffed with Ricotta, Romano, Provolone, Mozzarella Cheese, along with Eggs, Parsley and topped with a delicious Meat Sauce)	4.25
VEAL CUTLET ALA PARMIGIANO (Cutlet baked with cheese); A breaded cutlet, fried, then baked with Imported Provolone Cheese, and topped with a mild Tomato Sauce	4.25
BRASIOLA ROLLATINA (Rolled stuffed beef); Rolled beef, stuffed with garlic, parsley, celery, boiled eggs, and cheese, covered with a tempting Meat Sauce	4.75

Choice of Appetizers: Tomato Juice, Minestrone, or Italian Chicken Soup
Fresh Crisp Combination Salad, Coffee or Tea
Roquefort .25 extra *Sherbet*

Lentini's Steaks... Carefully Char-broiled--Perfect

CHOICE 12-OZ. T-BONE STEAK Choice of Potato	4.75
CHOICE 16-OZ. T-BONE STEAK Choice of Potato	5.25
LADIES CHOICE 8-OZ. DELMONICO STEAK Choice of Potato	3.95
CHOICE FILET MIGNON Choice of Potato	5.25
CHOICE NEW YORK STRIP SIRLOIN Choice of Potato	5.25
CHOPPED SIRLOIN STEAK Choice of Potato	2.65

Choice of Appetizers: Tomato Juice, Minestrone, or Italian Chicken Soup
Fresh Crisp Combination Salad, Coffee or Tea
Roquefort .25 extra

Desserts

SPUMONI	.50	CHEESE CAKE	.50
SHERBET	.30		

Beverages

COFFEE (with one warm-up)	.15	MILK	.20
TEA	.20	SOFT DRINKS	.20

May we suggest a fine wine, or brew, to accompany the selection you've made, or a cocktail for right now. Our list is on page one.

No alcoholic beverages sold to minors

Part of Lentini's menu. *Courtesy Michael Johman.*

crazy brothers." Wells and Grubb promised to return Lentini's "to its Italian roots and the unmatched attentive service that 'Sonny' Lentini historically provided." Sonny may have never envisioned "Soprano Sundays," where guests were invited to enjoy a meal and watch the HBO mobster series on a big-screen TV. The "Fratelli Oobatz" didn't stay owners for long, with Joe Thompson taking over in 2006. Thompson further reinforced Italian stereotypes by adding a small iron cart with photos of mobsters Lucky Luciano and Al Capone alongside a Thompson submachine gun menacingly reminding diners to make dinner reservations. *Courier-Journal* critic Sarah Fritschner enjoyed it in early 2007, saying that "Lentini's offers what it did four decades ago, a neighborhood spot with dependable food." However, in May 2008, food writer Marty Rosen celebrated the arrival of Jeff Jarfi and Jarfi's Bistro, noting that Lentini's, once "a bastion of Italian-American cuisine, classy enough for an anniversary party, accessible enough for a prom date," had its legacy "tarnished" by successors "who retained the name but none of the eatery's spirit." Phat Thanh Le returned not long after, reopening Cafe Mimosa along with a sister restaurant, The Egg Roll Machine. In 2010, Marty Rosen wrote that the dual restaurants focused on "risk-averse, Americanized takes on Vietnamese (the Café Mimosa side of the menu) and Chinese cuisine (The Egg Roll Machine)," featuring a "ubiquity" of televisions and a sushi bar.

The limestone-faced building with its arched windows still bears the signposts put up by Sonny Lentini. Perhaps wind, fire or other disaster will take them away, but for many in Louisville, nothing can tear down their memories of what many consider their favorite Italian place to dine.

18

Lynn's Paradise Cafe

CREATING A WORLD OF SWIRL WHERE THE CENTER CANNOT HOLD

In 2015, a group of about twenty protesters gathered around an empty storefront on Barret Avenue. Their signs urged the building owner to "Stop Holding Our Neighborhood Hostage" and "Move On" along with other, less friendly advice. Since the property became vacant, two neighboring businesses had closed, and people were growing tired of the vacant space with its paint-spalled concrete menagerie and giant coffee pot. In a Facebook post, one of the store owners thanked Lynn Winter for building such a successful business but sourly added, "Your legacy has been sullied by your actions and your unwillingness to act." Winter's unique blend of kitsch, good cooking and creative energy did leave a lasting legacy in Louisville. And despite the controversies swirling around its ending, Lynn's Paradise Cafe still remains one of Louisville's most memorable restaurants.

Winter returned to Louisville via California. She had spent several years working with Margaret Fox at Cafe Beaujolais, which at the time was the high point of every foodie's Mendocino pilgrimage. Born in Louisville, Winter went to grade school in Chicago and then moved back to Lexington, Kentucky. Graduating from Tates Creek High School, she spent the next four years making Shaker and primitive furniture but also working in restaurants. She thought about opening a restaurant in Lexington, but a place on Frankfort Avenue fit her fancy, and she opened her Paradise Cafe in 1991. Lynn's place served breakfast and lunch, along with a side of whimsy. Critics began to rave about the fresh buttermilk biscuits, homemade pork sausage, seven-grain porridge blend and, novel at the time, the "breakfast burrito" of spicy black beans, scrambled eggs, salsa, cheese and sour cream. Winter quickly expanded her hours to dinner, and plates containing spicy Thai beef rendang and house-roasted turkey dished up with real mashed potatoes and gravy were also well received. Lynn's decorations also got lots of attention. Tables were lit by 1950s-style reading lamps. The menu cover, actually a color copy of some boxer shorts Winter bought in California, pictured cutlery, bacon strips, sizzling eggs and steaming cups of coffee. The whimsy combined with solid cooking quickly became a city favorite.

Louisville Magazine food writer James Nold praised Lynn's as a "really good place to enjoy a home-cooked meal," adding that it was "right pathetic to think" that before Lynn's you could get great hummus in Louisville "but only mediocre meatloaf." Nold held special reverence for the Paradise Cafe's chicken pot pie with its fresh vegetables, roast chicken, from-scratch roux and homemade butter-flake crust. He also praised the kitchen for its interesting, seasonal vegetable dishes made from fresh ingredients, saying it made Lynn's "a special boon for local vegetarians." Meatloaf, breakfast burritos and pot pie quickly became Paradise Cafe standards, as did the Greek Scramble with black olives, feta cheese, diced tomatoes and sour cream.

The crowds kept coming, and Winter began thinking of a new home for her restaurant. In September 1993, she announced that she had found it at the site of the former Haberlin's Key Market on Barret Avenue. Winter purchased the Highlands building, saying, "It will be permanently mine so I can put my all into it." Working with architect Mark Hawkins, she added more windows and a dining counter as well as tables. She outlined her plans to decorate the parking lot with sculptures and add a gift shop with kitschy things for customers. "I want it to be a landmark," she said. Winter said she had no plans to change her original concept of a cozy, friendly neighborhood place that offers home-cooked food. "That's really important to me. And it'll be decorated hilariously. I have some great ideas for it." In 1994, the relocated Lynn's Paradise Cafe opened and began to make its mark on Barret Avenue.

Shortly after the reopening, *Courier-Journal* critic Susan Reigler wrote, "Business at the new and bigger Lynn's Paradise Cafe is so brisk that owner Lynn Winter hasn't had a chance to hang the eggs on the famous egg tree." Reigler also delighted in the new location's tin fluorescent light covers with breakfast appliances stenciled on them, a jungle mural on the wall of the hall leading to the restrooms and handmade colorful tiles depicting different foodstuffs at the diner-style bar. Reigler noted that, due to its popularity, "part of the experience of eating at Lynn's is the near-ritual wait for a table,"

Lynn's Paradise Cafe. *Courtesy Michelle Turner.*

pointing out that the parking lot, adorned with concrete animals and a giant red coffee pot fountain, and the larger waiting space inside both offered plenty of diversions while hanging around waiting for others to finish. Reigler was "heartened" to find all her Paradise favorites still on the menu: meatloaf, Chinese stir-fry, even the breakfast burrito. There were also some new items, including walnut-crusted chicken, lightly battered in crushed walnuts and herbs and fried and served with a honey Dijon mustard sauce.

The concrete animals and giant coffee pot were soon joined by a corn mural on the side of the building depicting "a breakfast scene." The large parking lot allowed for outside celebrations, including the "Derby Feast-o-Rama." Lynn's open-to-anyone party included live bluegrass music, free espresso and cappuccino, wooden-bowl carving demonstrations, free ice cream and vendors selling marinades, goat cheese and more. The multiple-day celebration offered visitors an instant photo taken with the Derby-winning horse (it was actually a person dressed in a horse costume sharing the Polaroid moment). Marking its sixth anniversary in 1997, Paradise Cafe served free breakfast or lunch to every six- and sixty-year-old guest, along with free cake and cappuccino. More outdoor dining space was added under a one-hundred-foot-long wisteria-covered pergola.

Left: A table set at Lynn's Paradise Cafe. *Courtesy John Nation.*

Below: Lynn Winter with some ugly lamps. *Courtesy John Nation.*

National media became increasingly interested in Winter and the Paradise Cafe. CBS News, the *New York Times* and other outlets featured Winter. She also garnered a two-page spread in *American Style* magazine, the editors showcasing her "funky-style art" and "new-wave comfort cuisine" along with a miniature diorama of the restaurant's interior. She participated in a "Conference on Corn" at the Smithsonian Institution's National Museum of American History and continued shifting the restaurant's corn mural theme through Muhammad Ali, Thoroughbred racing, basketball, baseball, hula dancers, palm trees and other creative expressions. Her contests, celebrations and, above all, good food kept bringing people in. In 1998, Winter again expanded out, bringing her ugly lamps to all of Kentucky.

The first Kentucky State Fair "Ugly Lamp Contest" netted Mary Charnes $500 for a red crushed-velvet lamp with black fringe and large, round bulbs above a brass base. More than seventy people entered, and hundreds of people watched the judging while thousands more had the opportunity to ogle some of the commonwealth's ugliest lighting fixtures. Winter said she dreamt up the contest after Kentucky State Fair officials asked her to help with a poultry-dressing contest. "I didn't know anyone who dressed their poultry up, so I asked them if I could come up with my own contest," said Winter. "I was sitting in the restaurant near an ugly, crushed green velvet lamp, and I said I want to do an ugly lamp contest." The fair contest ran until 2013, attracting oddly decorated lamps from as far away as Europe, and it continued to spread Lynn's ideas of fun and whimsy.

As the century turned, Winter's popularity and projects continued to expand along with the Paradise Cafe's staff and menu. Chef Michael Captain introduced a flaming saganaki appetizer. Winter directed the transformation of a space in the Glassworks building into a jazz club. In 2002, the Paradise Cafe earned a place as one of *Esquire*'s "Four Most Fun Restaurants in America," with food writer John Mariani crediting the corncob-and-conch-shell mural, the coffee pot fountain and "a dining room decked out like 'Pee-wee's Playhouse'" for "some of the best Southern cooking, biscuits, omelets and meatloaf dinners you'll ever eat." It was around this time that the Paradise Cafe entered "The World of Swirl."

In 2003, Winter announced that she was transforming the former front waiting area into a store full of "fun swirly things." While waiting for a table or just stopping by, shoppers could contemplate buying steak-shaped air fresheners that smelled of barbecued meat, purses made from sewn-together juice pouches, extendable "freeloader forks" and other whimsical items. Calling the shop a "genre-buster," Winter also introduced her own merchandise. She wrote and published *The Birth of Swirl*, a book she described as "fairy tales for the young and young at heart." In the book, Piper the Penguin, Frilled Lizard and other characters had adventures that let them "stretch beyond what they think they are." She also offered "Magic Pants" in a variety of metallic, animal print, see-through and retro wash-and-wear patterns. Winter told a *Courier-Journal* reporter that the World of Swirl was less about increasing profit and more about "intensifying the unique experience of Lynn's…to create a 'Wow' you don't get anywhere else in the world." It didn't hurt that the fake lizards, bottletop-studded belts and other ephemera had increased restaurant sales 15 percent.

The media attention kept growing and Lynn made *Bon Appétit Magazine*'s "100 Best Neighborhood Restaurants" list, appeared on Oprah Winfrey's show and sparred with Chef Bobby Flay. Business kept booming, and neighborhood businesses such as Nuts and Stuff and the Regalo Gifts shop began to profit off the increased traffic The Swirl had brought to Barret Avenue. Bill and Hillary Clinton stopped by for a photo-op before the primary election of 2008, Mrs. Clinton mingling with the patrons while Mr. Clinton held an impromptu press briefing near the kitchen door. Things seemed to be steadily, whimsically wonderful. Restaurant critic Marty Rosen lauded Lynn's "well-deserved national reputation as a bastion of the great American breakfast," adding that "seldom has a restaurant managed to cram as much zany, colorful weirdness within four walls." Some of the "zany, wonderful weirdness" would seemingly become part of a darker story in just a few years—a story that finally brought an end to Paradise.

In January 2012, the group Kentucky Jobs with Justice, along with several former and current employees of Lynn's, began distributing pamphlets challenging what they perceived as a hostile working environment. They claimed that employees suffered verbal abuse and harassment and were subject to a requirement that all servers had to possess a minimum of $100 cash while at work. The complaints broke after former server Leila DiFazio posted on Facebook, claiming she lost her job for failing to keep $100 on hand and asking people to "Please, please, PLEASE join me in making this right and/or exposing the madness within 'Paradise.'" The website Eater picked up on DiFazio's story. Winter defended herself by claiming she established the $100 rule to protect "the secondarily tipped people (buses, bartenders, foodrunners and expos) because…[she] didn't want them to say 'I have no cash, I can't tip you today.'" Eater published an article questioning the legality of Lynn's policies. Soon after, five negative accounts claiming to be from former Lynn's employees appeared on Service Workers for Justice, a website backed by Kentucky Jobs with Justice. "Far from Paradise: The Story Behind Lynn's Café," included statements such as "My time at LPC was the most Kafkaesque experience under a Machiavellian reign of terror" and "It took me months to become financially stable again and I'm still trying to deal emotionally and psychologically with everything I experienced there." The group of current and former Lynn's employees demanded a reversal of the "$100 bank" policy and the rehiring of employees who were fired for speaking out against the policy. As the media attention grew, Winter abruptly announced she was shutting down Lynn's Paradise Cafe, the restaurant's Facebook page posting later that "Lynn is moving on from Paradise and on to her next crazy adventure. She's scouring the universe for the perfect next owner of Lynn's who will not only carry on its legacy but also make it more awesomer!"

The universe is a very large place, and scouring it seemed to take an awful lot of time. Initially, Lynn insisted that any prospective buyers "must agree to carry on the restaurant's quirky tradition" and hinted she could still be part of a future operation. But the months dragged on, and neighboring businesses began to close, leaving the Barret Avenue neighborhood once again beleaguered and its residents beginning to complain. Finally, in 2016, Lynn announced that she had sold the property. With two weeks to clear out the former Paradise Cafe, she declared that she would give everything away. Concrete animal statues, the giant red teapot, dozens of ugly lamps, fake moustaches, T-shirts, coffee mugs and other psychedelic swag would be awarded to winners of an online contest. Winter said she would keep only two items: a table lamp made from a stuffed armadillo and another lamp made out of a stuffed white squirrel. After twenty-two years of breakfast burritos, bourbon ball milkshakes, egg trees and ugly lamps, Lynn's Paradise Cafe was coming to an end. Winter told *Courier-Journal* reporter Jere Downs that she closed the restaurant "amid a personal and health crisis."

A branch of a barbecue outlet finally replaced the former Paradise Cafe. The World of Swirl is gone. The animals, murals and other signs of the Paradise Cafe no longer remain. But as Lynn herself said, "What a wild and spectacular dream we held in place." At least, for as long as she could hold onto it.

Pecan-Crusted Chicken

Lynn's recipes were frequently requested by *Courier-Journal* readers. Ron Mikulak provided a version of this popular chicken dish in a 2010 "Cooks Corner" column.

6 boneless, skinless chicken breasts
1 cup buttermilk
¼ cup (or more) vegetable oil
4 cups all-purpose flour
2 cups pecans
¼ cup kosher salt
4 pieces bacon
¼ cup minced shallots
3 tablespoons all-purpose flour
½ cup maple syrup
⅓ cup whole-grain Creole mustard
1 teaspoon Dijon mustard
1 teaspoon kosher salt
⅓ cup Woodford Reserve bourbon
2 cups heavy cream

Place chicken breasts in a plastic bag or other container with the buttermilk and marinate for at least 3 hours or overnight in the refrigerator. Heat oil in a skillet over medium heat, sprinkling in a pinch of flour, which will bubble when the oil comes to the right temperature. Coarsely chop pecans and mix with flour and salt. Remove chicken from marinade, allowing excess buttermilk to drip off. Dredge chicken in pecan flour. Put the breasts in the skillet, being careful not to overcrowd the pan. Depending on the size of the breasts, cook for about 4 minutes on each side until juices run clear. Arrange cooked breasts on a serving plate. Spoon bourbon cream sauce over the chicken and serve.

Bourbon cream sauce: Chop bacon in ¼-inch dice and fry in a large saucepan until crisp. Remove bacon and save for garnish. Over medium heat, sauté shallots in bacon fat until translucent. Add flour and stir for 2 minutes. Add syrup, mustards, salt and bourbon and cook until thickened. Stir in cream and simmer for 3 to 5 minutes until desired consistency is reached.

Lynn's Paradise Cafe Meatloaf

1 pound ground beef
½ pound ground pork
2 slices white bread, cubed
1 onion, diced
4 cloves garlic, diced
1 teaspoon dried thyme
1 teaspoon dried sage
1 tablespoon hot sauce
2 large eggs, beaten
1 tablespoon Worcestershire sauce
salt and pepper

Preheat oven to 350°. Combine spices, sauces and eggs. Pour mixture over meat and blend. Add bread cubes and gently fold in until mixed. Form into a loaf and place into a lightly greased baking dish. Bake for about 1 hour or until done. Serves 6 to 8.

19

Min's East End Cafe

THE "DIRTY" LITTLE SECRET BEHIND A LEGENDARY STEAKHOUSE

Eighteen thousand bushels of green beans, strung by hand on the front stoop; at least two bushels every afternoon, six days a week. That was only part of what Minnie Perryman Kohler managed to do in over thirty-five years of serving food to Louisvillians at what became known as "Dirty Min's"—because Kohler also launched one of Louisville's most notable steakhouses.

Min was born Minnie Morrison in a home only a few blocks from what became her Story Avenue restaurant. Green beans seem to have always been a part of her life. She began picking beans and digging potatoes at a River Road farm owned by a relative. In 1932, she opened a restaurant and filling station on River Road, selling a large ribeye steak with tomatoes for fifteen cents. That steak place was wiped out by the 1937 flood, which left Min (along with many other waterlogged Louisvillians) looking for a new place. Min's East End Cafe opened in Butchertown in 1938, and Min began stringing beans and peeling potatoes by the front entrance rather than the kitchen, which occupied most of the narrow cafe's front room. Patrons had to walk past steam tables, tubs of beans and potatoes, giant coffee urns and busy cook staff on their way to the back, where they could drink, eat and play cards. Veal cutlets were on the menu for a dime, with a plate lunch costing only a quarter. Homemade soups included vegetable, bean, chicken noodle and chili.

In 1958, Min decided to make Louisville choose between two Min's restaurants. She opened Min's Steak House on Brownsboro Road, with an ad

Min's East End menu cover. *Courtesy Michael Johmann.*

declaring "Steaks Our Specialty" seven days a week. Min's East End continued to offer an array of dishes to go along with her hand-strung beans. A 1967 menu boasted breakfast, lunch and dinner along with an array of local beers. Shrimp cocktail, country ham, pan-fried oysters (in season), hamburgers, pork chops and even New York and sirloin strip steaks were available, leading understandably to some confusion between the two Min's. People began to refer to the Brownsboro steakhouse as "Min's," while the East End Cafe became known to locals as "Dirty Min's." This may have been after 1972, when Kentucky's Department for Health Services outlawed the kind of kitchen where customers could "walk through and be talking, chewing gum, sneezing and coughing." The original East End Cafe was old enough to avoid the new code, but it may have reinforced the "dirty" idea of the still-popular small place.

Min decided to stop stringing beans and retired shortly after the death of her bartending brother Clarence in 1973. The growing number of fast-food places, lack of parking on a one-way street and possibly the "dirty" name meant the people who took over had a harder time than Min, who continued to wave at customers from her nearby home. In 1985, the Francis family changed the name of what was now their restaurant to Pat's. (Min sold the property to the Francis family in 1988, having leased it to them before that.) In 1989, after fifty years, Min's East End Cafe announced that it would close.

A string of restaurants followed in Min's wake, none of them lasting anywhere near a half century. The elaborate sign Min put over the simple Story Avenue structure is still there, now bearing the name "Fusion Restaurant." Look closely, however and you will see how the white-painted blocks above "Fusion" barely cover the letters *M I N S*. The beans may be gone, but the strong lady who strung them still looms over Story Avenue.

20

Mozz

FRESHLY MADE CHEESE MELTS DOWN ALL TOO QUICKLY

The buzz in 2010 was almost breathless as Casa Grisanti alumni Michael Cooper and Matthew Antonovich announced their plans for a new restaurant, Mozz. Arriving in Louisville in the late 1980s, Antonovich had a resume that included working for Wolfgang Puck, Dean Fearing and "other American food luminaries." When Casa closed in 1991, Antonovich was the legendary Italian restaurant's executive chef. He then took on the position of chef for Grisanti's chain of casual restaurants before moving to Dallas, where he operated a series of restaurants before returning to Louisville. Communicating with Antonovich, who he'd known for many years, food writer Steve Coomes reported on the chef's inclusion of a "European-style" dining room, a two-hundred-seat jazz bar and a thirty-four-foot white marble counter where chefs would prepare fresh mozzarella every hour. Expanding the Cobalt Building space formerly occupied by Primo to nearly ten thousand square feet, Antonovich used artisan glass, Italian furniture and "an abundant use of stainless steel" to create what *Courier-Journal* critic Nancy Miller described as "Milan meets Japan." She also praised the restaurant's Mozzarella Bar and porcini-crusted ribeye. In just a few months, the massive place at the corner of Market and Jackson was named "best new restaurant" by the readers of *Louisville Magazine*. That same July, Coomes called Mozz "a serious restaurant with more than enough merits to deserve the honor."

As Mozz continued to succeed, Antonovich attracted more investors, who decided the chef should also helm a restaurant at Fourth Street

Left: Matthew Antonovich pulling mozzarella. *Courtesy Dan Dry/*Food & Dining Magazine.

Below: Mozz interior. *Courtesy Dan Dry/*Food & Dining Magazine.

Live. The two-hundred-seat Mozzaria opened on May 2, 2012. It was announced as "an ambitious culinary combination of gastro-pub, New York-style delicatessen, pizzeria, burger grill, pasta house and souvenir shop." Instead, it became the cause of Antonovich's exit from the Louisville culinary scene and seemingly cracked the code of silence around many problems Mozz had been having.

A Jefferson Circuit Court complaint filed by investor Matthew Salzman about nine weeks after Mozzaria's May opening alleged that Antonovich had been "making unauthorized payments…[and] diverting assets to another business he manages in which he has an ownership stake," reportedly Mozz. It turned out that Mozz, as well as Mozzaria, had been so spotty in paying vendors that the restaurants had been placed on a "cash on demand" list. By August 2012, Antonovich was out, and Steve Coomes began to release more details about what had been going on behind the scenes. Michael Cooper told Coomes that while he still owned a third of the restaurant, he wasn't sure Mozz was still open, adding that Antonovich's mismanagement was "tough on our friendship." By September 2012, Mozz was gone—but Coomes felt that some more dirt should be shoveled on the grave.

Despite his earlier descriptions of Mozz as "a serious restaurant," Coomes claimed he always knew Mozz "was a sketchy venture, at best, from the start." Coomes divulged that he had contacted Nancy Nichols, a writer for Dallas's *D Magazine*, who warned Coomes that Antonovich was "trouble." After the closing, Coomes also detailed his skepticism of Mozz's claim to "Vera Pizza Napoletana" certification and Antonovich's "mercurial moods," stiffing suppliers and "lofty claims that no one in the industry believed possible." As 2012 ended, *Insider Louisville* published what it referred to as "a cautionary tale," wherein Steve Coomes reported how Antonovich's investors somehow never seemed to hear anything but positive feedback, despite Mozz's kitchen being "called everything from 'Louisville's own Hell's Kitchen' to 'a daily episode of the Maury Povich Show.'" Pallas Partners, the "reluctant" owners of Mozzaria, decided the restaurant's reputation was "too damaged" and changed the name to Quattro.

Antonovich moved on, opening at least one more restaurant in Franklin, Tennessee, before shifting his attention to real estate. The local food writers have moved on as well, perhaps a bit chastened as they remember celebrating the arrival of a big cheese, only to have it all melt away before their eyes.

Spaghetti Aglio Antonovich

Courier-Journal food editor Sarah Fritschner featured Antonovich's simple pasta dish in 1990.

1 cup olive oil
3 cloves or more garlic, crushed
1 teaspoon crushed red pepper flakes
minced fresh parsley
2 pounds dried spaghetti
½ to 1 cup Parmesan cheese
black pepper, freshly ground

Heat olive oil and add garlic, red pepper and parsley. As the garlic browns, discard the crushed cloves. Keep oil warm while bringing salted water to a boil. Add spaghetti to water and cook according to package directions. Drain spaghetti and put pasta into a serving bowl. Pour oil over spaghetti and sprinkle on cheese and freshly ground black pepper. Toss well and serve.

21

Myra's

FORMALLY (OR FORMERLY) FOSTERING LOUISVILLE'S BISTRO SCENE

"This is the old Myra's Grill, dressed up and gone fancy on us," wrote *Courier-Journal* reviewer John Finley in 1980 shortly after Tim Barnes opened Formally Myra's at Grinstead and Ray Avenue. A grill operated by Myra Rinker and her husband, Mervyn, had been in business at that address since at least the 1940s, offering what they advertised as "quality food at reasonable prices, served in our atmosphere of friendliness, specializing in chicken-steak dinners and those good old homemade pies." It seemed just about everyone in Louisville had something they liked about Myra's Grill, especially the banana cream and chess pies. But as the 1980s arrived, the Rinkers retired, and a different "atmosphere of friendliness" began to acquaint Louisville with a new concept: the American bistro.

These days, there are dozens of Louisville "bistros," including Asian, southern and Bourbon. Bistros first arose in France sometime in the 1800s, in some stories from Russians shouting *bistrot* (hurry), while others trace the term to the French word *bistouille*, meaning "bad wine." Either way, bistros became known for their casual, quick service, inexpensive wine and simple, hearty food, a concept that in 1980 was mostly new to Louisville. Tim Barnes thought it was past time to remedy that situation.

Barnes, who had come to Louisville from western Kentucky in the 1970s, had already made waves with his first restaurant, J. Timothy's, in the Mayflower Hotel on Ormsby Avenue. After closing J. Timothy's, Barnes purchased Myra's Grill from the retiring Rinkers. He remodeled and enlarged the former grill, removing the Formica tables and replacing the

Joanne and Bim Deitrich at Myra's. *Courtesy John Nation.*

soda fountain with a bar. He painted the ceiling black and the walls clay red with swathes of gray. Menus offered choucroute and chocolate mousse instead of chicken breast sandwiches and banana cream pie. "Bar-B-Qued Shrimp," marinated then broiled and served with a smoke-flavored sauce, was said to be the house specialty. The dessert menu did have chess pie, the standard from the old Myra's, one of the only things still linking the Rinkers to the location.

The new Myra's started to become something of an "in" spot, its then-novel wine bar offering nearly twenty wines by the glass. But while there were enough good meals to keep people coming in, critics began to complain that Barnes's food often failed to match the standards of what had been Myra's Grill. In 1982, Barnes turned to restaurateur Bim Deitrich, who had already been involved with successful ventures such as the Normandy Inn and the Bristol Bar & Grill. One of the first things Deitrich did as a partner was change the name. In a city where people still give directions based on places that no longer exist, the name "Formally Myra's" ran into some understandable confusion, with many people thinking the name was "Formerly Myra's"—the *Courier-Journal* included. Deitrich saw the "Formally" name as a problem, saying that even when they got it right, the name "confused people, and some thought they were actually supposed to wear a tuxedo." Deitrich convinced Barnes to change the name to "Myra's Ristorante," shift the dominant colors from red and gray to beige and change the menu. New dishes included pasta and burgers, along with more exotic items like a Moroccan veal ragout and shrimp and black-bean sauce. The burgers were popular, partly due to their "Famous Sauce" blending mayo, ketchup, chili powder and cumin. The most expensive item on the menu was Steak Diane, at $12.50, and Myra's kept earning praise as a moderately priced restaurant with consistently memorable food.

Barnes and Deitrich both had plans that meant Myra's could not continue, however. The success of Myra's and their own entrepreneurial energy meant that both men wanted to pursue other ideas. Deitrich left to open his eponymous restaurant in the old Crescent Theater, while Barnes opened the legendary Timothy's with its zebra-print wall. Myra's space became part of an expanded Burger's market. After helping introduce Louisville to the idea of bistros, what had become Formally Myra's had finally become formerly.

Myra's Chess Pie

In 1949, Cissy Gregg, legendary "Home Consultant" to the *Courier-Journal*, wrote that Myra's Grill's chess pie was "one of the best... [she] ever tasted." Gregg found this surprising given the relatively small number of eggs involved but insisted, "My, it's good!"

½ cup (one stick) butter or margarine, softened
1 ½ cups granulated sugar
3 whole eggs
1 teaspoon corn meal
1 teaspoon vanilla
1 teaspoon vinegar
8-inch or 9-inch pastry crust

Beat together butter or margarine, sugar and whole eggs. When combined, sprinkle on cornmeal, pour in vanilla and vinegar and beat in. Pour mixture into a pastry-lined pie pan. Bake at 375° for 30 minutes or until filling has set. Can also be baked in a 9-inch pie pan, but filling will not be as thick.

Myra's "Famous" Hamburger Sauce

On the eightieth anniversary of the cheeseburger in 1984, *Courier-Journal* food editor Elaine Corn published this recipe for the sauce accompanying Myra's hamburgers, noting that the sauce was "served in a small porcelain ramekin for dipping or spreading all over the burger."

2 cups mayonnaise
⅓ cup ketchup
2 tablespoons chili powder
2 tablespoons ground cumin

Combine ingredients. Keep chilled until ready to serve with hamburgers.

22

Normandy Inn

CREATING A SENSATION WHILE KEEPIN' ON TRUCKIN'

What happens when one young man puts his job on the line for a dream? Normandy Inn is what happens." That was how Paul O'Brien announced the opening of his restaurant, asserting in a newspaper ad that "the opening of Normandy Inn is more than just a personal triumph for its thirty-year-old owner. It's a victory for the entire city." O'Brien's "triumph" for Louisville was a remodeled and refurbished nineteenth-century riverfront building at Seventh and Washington Streets. Known as the Normandy Hotel before a fire gutted the upper part of the building and left it vacant in 1958, it had also been part of an iron foundry, a general-merchandise store, a saloon and (according to unofficial records) a "bawdy house." O'Brien kept the wrought-iron balconies on the second and third floors, adding stained-glass windows to the wall facing Seventh Street. Creating an interior of "curiously appealing and inviting rustic elegance, stimulating to rich conversation and warm friendship" took gold leaf lanterns, ornate French mirrors, bentwood chairs and "an antique telephone from Germany," among other things. While seemingly boastful, O'Brien did turn the Normandy into enough of a success that it could help subsidize another part of his life. In addition to his duties as restaurateur, O'Brien spent more and more time as a long-haul truck driver.

"Paul was from Philadelphia—Main Line," says Bim Deitrich, who had been hired by O'Brien for his first job in Louisville restaurants. Referring to O'Brien's upper-crust family, Deitrich said, "He was kind of a black sheep, I believe, or at least he used to purport that he was." Before he

Wine list cover from The Normandy Inn. *Courtesy Michael Johmann.*

owned the Normandy, O'Brien had managed food services at several institutions, including North Carolina State University, Union College in Barbourville, Southern Baptist Theological Seminary and Bellarmine College. He followed the Normandy Inn a few years later with the Hearthstone Tavern next door. Wearing a suit and tie, the genial, blue-eyed O'Brien would tackle personnel problems, approve menus, greet customers and meet with other downtown business merchants as he shepherded the success of both of his establishments. But, as Deitrich put it, after wearing the suit for a while, O'Brien would "then go 'ah, fuck it' and go get the truck."

O'Brien called his trucking "a hobby." But he made a considerable financial investment in a line of trucks and spent lots of time on the road. By 1974, he was riding in a shiny red Peterbilt with a leather interior, sometimes pulling a forty-foot refrigerated trailer. On the road, O'Brien was a smokier, sweatier and much less dressy version of his Normandy Inn self. And the food was a world away. As O'Brien told a *Louisville Times* reporter over a greasy, pallid plate at a truck stop in Virginia, he felt there were two ways of eating: "a fine meal with good food, good service, nice atmosphere. And things like this [truck stop meal]. This is just to fill my stomach."

O'Brien enjoyed juxtaposing his two avocations, said Deitrich, who left Normandy Inn in 1977 along with some partners to open the Bristol. Deitrich added that O'Brien enjoyed the idea that his truck driving might shock the sophisticated "ladies who lunch," and O'Brien continued doing interviews and radio shows detailing his life as a truck driver. But his highway journeys may have taken the focus away from his flagship restaurant.

In 1969, the Normandy Inn's menu floridly presented prime rib, "robust, heavy steer sirloin steak," lamb chops, Dover sole and "Poulet Fantastique," a "properly boned breast of an excellent chicken, over old and tender country ham, adorned with sauce Chausseur." Also promised were "magnificent sandwiches" in The Den, a subterranean "English-style" pub complete with a low, exposed-beam ceiling. In 1972, *Courier-Journal* critic Richard Des Ruisseaux declared Normandy's relish tray of corn, marinated artichoke hearts and "a potpourri of pickled pimentoes" part of his dream meal at a fantasy Louisville restaurant. But by 1978, critic Paul Neely complained that, while Normandy's menu and pleasant atmosphere made an evening there seem promising, "the promises start to turn sour." Neely's "Le Canard a l'Orange Curaçao" and "Superb red snapper Grand Duc" didn't live up to their overwrought descriptions. The duck was "tougher and certainly dryer than it should have been," and the snapper was topped by something that looked, felt and tasted like "congealed white paste." Neely bemoaned that, while Normandy Inn had been "one of the places to go in Louisville" for several years, the restaurant was coasting on its past record.

In 1979, O'Brien announced that the Normandy Inn and the Hearthstone Tavern were closed and up for sale. He continued on with his trucking business, appearing to talk about "Life on the Road" with radio host Milton Metz in January 1983. But the following June, O'Brien's life on the road was cut short. It was not noted whether he was driving the red, thirteen-speed "luxury" Peterbilt truck, but while heading east on Indiana Highway 62 near Chelsea, O'Brien swerved to avoid a drunk driver who had pulled out of an intersection into his path. The truck hit the car, flipped over and skidded several hundred feet. O'Brien was pronounced dead at the scene.

"Paul was a creative guy, for sure," says Bim Deitrich, recalling how O'Brien saw the opportunity at the crumbling corner of Seventh and Washington. "It was a real loss. Doug Gossman [of the Bristol] and I, Nancy Shepherd [of Cafe Metro], we came after Paul....Paul was the first to modernize, but in an antique way." Louisville will never know what other ideas O'Brien may have had in store for the city. But we will always owe a little something to the truck driver who saw potential in the West Main District.

23

Parisian Pantry

BREAD RISING HELPS REVIVE BARDSTOWN ROAD

By 1984, Louisville had begun to notice that business on Bardstown Road was changing. Richard O'Malley, president of Bardstown Road Tomorrow, noted that for a number of years people hadn't wanted to visit Bardstown Road "because it was dirty, it was hard to find parking, and the businesses were kind of grungy looking." But as Cafe Metro, Swanson Gallery and other upscale ventures began to flourish, people began to see the potential in something new, chic and different along Bardstown Road. Among them was the Whitaker family, who brought to town what many Louisvillians at the time considered the best bread in the city.

After leaving an attorney position in 1982, Julia Whitaker sat down with her two sons and shared with them her idea about opening a French bakery and restaurant. Michael, then attending college in Montpellier, France, was a big supporter, as was Richard, who had worked and cooked in restaurants. Michael found a French couple interested in discussing a partnership, and Julia Whitaker traveled to France in May 1983, returning with what she believed was a French connection that would help the Whitakers open their establishment at the corner of Bardstown and Bonnycastle.

In addition to investor money, the Whitakers also returned from France with a baker. Jean-Yves Joret had grown up working in his family's bakery in Livarot, a village in Normandy known for Calvados brandy and a soft, pungent cheese. The Whitakers started tearing down walls and buying equipment, and then the French investor couple decided they wanted their money back. Julia found some other financing through three friends who

Baguettes at Parisian Pantry. *Courtesy John Nation.*

became limited partners, and the Parisian Pantry opened its doors in June 1984. Almost immediately, the bread became a hit. In July, the *Courier-Journal*'s Jack Roby called it "the finest bread I've eaten in Louisville." Unfortunately, he added, "I only wish the accolades could continue with the food." Roby thought his fish was "not so fresh" and overcooked, his cassoulet overloaded with beans with a miserly ration of "sausages that no French charcuterie has ever sold" and his dessert disappointing. In the end, however, he encouraged others to visit Parisian Pantry, saying that he would choose Joret's bread "above all other breads available locally."

The imbalance between Parisian Pantry's bread and broader offerings continued to be noted by critics. In 1986, *Courier-Journal* reporter Marilyn McCraven criticized Parisian Pantry's entrees, saying that she hoped "the chef spices up his act." The underperforming kitchen didn't stop Parisian Pantry's reputation from growing. In 1987, the Galleria asked the Whitakers to open an outlet for the holiday season. Jean-Yves Joret appeared at benefits around town, serving baked goods to delighted attendees. But the holiday season would also bring the Whitakers regret for some of their involvement with France. In December, a jury ruled that the Whitakers had never returned their former French partners' $25,000 initial investment and owed them that amount plus $14,000 in interest. In February 1987, the Whitakers filed for debt protection under Chapter 11. Relatives Michael and Georgia Whitaker stepped in along with baker Joret to keep Parisian Pantry afloat, helped by a last-minute lease extension from the property owner. The menu was expanded, and some prices were lowered. Richard Whitaker left for another restaurant, but Jean-Yves continued to give the city some great bread. The food, however, remained a problem. In 1989, critic Robin Garr extolled the "feather-light, chewy-crust French country white bread" from the Pantry, writing that, along with the loaves, the art deco light fixtures and green storefront awnings allowed him to "squint my eyes and pretend I'm in Paris" but that, "unfortunately, dinner fails to maintain the illusion." Garr thought that his *potage parmentier*, chicken Dijonais and other entrées seemed "to have been prepared by someone who is cooking because he has to, not because he wants to." Then something worse than mediocre food appeared at Parisian Pantry—the U.S. Immigration service, demanding Jean-Yves Joret return to France.

In 1990, after Joret had left, Debbie Taylor and Barry Yates bought the Parisian Pantry. Taylor had been a corporate trainer for T.G.I. Fridays, while Yates had been general manager for Ferd Grisanti. The new owners introduced a menu featuring "light fare, pasta dishes and appetizers—all prepared with a European flair." Instead of Joret, the Parisian Pantry brought in Deanna Rushing, who had previously baked at the Pantry with Joret. Critics were not very kind. Ronni Lundy found that the baked goods had "fallen in quality" and thought the new menu was "too ambitious," even the "hollowed pumpernickel boule stuffed with that salty, creamy spinach dip ubiquitous at parties around town." But in January 1992, his immigration problems solved, Jean-Yves Joret returned, and the Parisian Pantry celebrated. The Pantry's bakery business, which had declined in the interim, tripled on his return. The restaurant promoted Joret in advertisements, even printing T-shirts with the slogan "The King Is Back." Debbie Taylor celebrated the new business, saying, "even the restaurant's doing better—I think it's because people think Jean-Yves cooks too."

But the illusion of Joret's competence flowing into the kitchen must have soon worn off; by 1994, the Parisian Pantry had been sold to Michael and Caren Yarmuth, who changed the name to Parisian Cafe and continued to both employ Joret and receive bad reviews about the food. In 1995, saying he "never imagined that running a restaurant would be so time-consuming or tiring," Michael Yarmuth announced that the Parisian Cafe would close. "I'm in my 50s and it was just too much to try and keep up," he added. Joret moved on to another bakery and then other professions. Today, Louisville has several options for French breads. But the small place on Bardstown Road will long be remembered for bringing good baguettes to the city named for a French king and adding to the route's reputation as Louisville's "Restaurant Row."

Vinaigrette Dressing

Alice Colombo provided Richard Whitaker's vinaigrette recipe in a 1986 *Courier-Journal* "Cooks Corner."

2½ cups neutral oil
½ cup olive oil
1 cup champagne vinegar
2 teaspoons Dijon mustard
3 tablespoons finely minced onion
1 teaspoon marjoram
1 teaspoon thyme

1 teaspoon basil
½ teaspoon oregano
1 tablespoon chopped fresh parsley

Put all ingredients into a food processor, blender or tight-lidded jar. Blend well. Shake again before serving.

24

The Rudyard Kipling

BURGOO AND BANDS BUILDING A PEACEABLE KINGDOM

A place for folks of various ages, sexes, colors, pockets, hairstyles, etc., to meet and eat and listen to music and talk and appreciate and grow." It may not seem like such a radical idea in Louisville today. But in the 1960s, when Sheila and Ken Pyle began uniting music and meals, the city wasn't quite as enlightened.

Ken Pyle came to Louisville to attend the Southern Baptist Theological Seminary after a baseball scholarship paid for his philosophy degree from Rice University. In 1966, he met and married Sheila after the couple had been spending time together at The Shack, a Bardstown Road hangout near the Mid-City Mall. Sheila grew up in Madison County, Kentucky, before earning a BA in English from Berea College and a master's degree in theater from the University of Kentucky. In the late 1960s, the Mid-City Mall area was heavy with head shops patronized by rough characters like the Outlaws motorcycle gang. Undeterred, the newlywed Pyles bought The Shack, renaming it the Roundtable Theater. They hosted local singers, Louisville Peace Council meetings and eastern Kentucky poverty workers while serving whole-grain breads, burgoo and beer cheese. Sheila recalled to music writer Leslie Stewart how the Roundtable's progressive bent meant they were "persecuted and regarded with horror," including a ludicrous rumor accusing the Pyles of flying the North Vietnamese flag (it was actually the flag of Texas, Ken Pyle's home state). When a storm demolished the Roundtable sign, Ken and Sheila decided it was time to redo the entire club, this time rechristening it as the Storefront Congregation.

Ken and Sheila cooked, washed the fruit-jar beer mugs, cleaned and kept order at the Storefront and continued with their friendly reminders that around Louisville there were people some might consider "weird." The Pyles tucked messages into every menu, such as, "If you are not intimidated by inconsistency, distressed by dichotomy, or scared by schizophrenia, if instead you feel confounded by conformity and stultified by sameness, piqued by pigeon-holing and negated by niches—you will receive aid and comfort." The Storefront served up soup beans, Kentucky ham, whole-wheat biscuits, gumbo, burgoo, sassafras tea and Irish stew while hosting theater groups, gospel singers and musicians, including the legendary Ralph Stanley.

The Pyles closed the Storefront Congregation in 1974, moving to Berea with their three children to care for Sheila's ailing father. When they returned to Louisville in the early 1980s, Bardstown Road real estate values had risen, so Ken and Sheila could not afford to reopen the Storefront Congregation in its old location. They began searching for a new spot, settling on a split-level building near the corner of Fourth and Oak Streets. The Pyles wanted a name they felt would fit into the Old Louisville setting, would tell customers they could "expect menus from all over the world" and would be distinctive and English. They went through list after list of names for several months before Sheila, as she later told *Courier-Journal* reporter Dick Kaukas, heard a "very rich and deep" voice bellow "RUD-YARD! KIP-LING!" Deciding that the disembodied voice had the final say, Ken and Sheila named the place for the famous British author, and after two years of renovation, the Rudyard Kipling opened in January 1985 under signs featuring two kissing elephants. One large, airy room could accommodate about one hundred people for musical performances, while a few steps down and to the right, a bar and dining room were large enough for about sixty people. Ken Pyle told a reporter that he wanted the place to have "an English-pub kind of atmosphere," but that idea went someplace else almost immediately. The decor featured a bust of Rudyard Kipling, Japanese lanterns, a huge stuffed elephant, stained-glass windows and brightly colored animal prints. Patrons began bringing in other elephants, adding to an ever-growing collection on the bar. Wooden lattice work, flower prints and ceiling fans created a "gazebo-like" atmosphere, and the food was well received by critics.

In 1986, the *Courier-Journal*'s Jack Roby found the scope of the Pyles' menu "a bit difficult to comprehend," with "health-food" items like a fresh fruit frappe to "not so healthy dishes like country ham and corn pones." But his overall impression was that "if the foods continue on the same level…this Rudyard Kipling should be around for a long time." Others

Ken and Sheila Pyle. *Courtesy John Nation.*

noted how quickly the Rudyard Kipling became "a favorite hangout for a diverse collection of interesting people" in an era where Louisville's yuppie fern-bar scene was expanding. Diners could enjoy traditional Kentucky burgoo, red beans and rice, "English-style pub pies," roast pork or a "Shake Shake Shake" made with lowfat milk, protein and vitamin supplements. What went hand-in-hand with the diverse menu was the diverse entertainment, helping turn "The Rud" into one of Louisville's most eclectic and embraced music spaces.

Dick Kaukas's description of a "fairly typical" evening at The Rud in 1992 included a band called Top Hat Magna Carta, Ken Pyle playing darts, a woman reading and eating quietly by herself and four men taking shots of one-hundred-proof Rumple Minze at the bar while another recited his poem "If Harlem Were But a Woman" nearby. Groups of friends would gather on Friday nights for singalongs. People came to the Pyles' place to watch plays, drink, argue, hug friends, make friends and many combinations in between. And, of course, they came to listen to music.

"The Rudyard Kipling books from more genres of Louisville music than any other venue I could name," musician Alan Canon told Leslie Stewart in 2003. On any given night, the sounds of bluegrass, blues, jazz, folk, reggae, African, traditional Irish or jam-session combinations of any of these could be heard, along with poetry and avant-garde theater. Phish, Love Jones, My Morning Jacket, the Black Keys and other groups appeared at the Oak Street venue. One reason performers liked The Rud was Ken Pyle's nontraditional management approach, which allowed artists to determine their own cover charges and keep whatever they collected at the door. It wasn't the most profitable way to run a business, but the music community returned the favor when The Rudyard Kipling was so financially threatened that it was faced with losing its liquor license. Folk, blues, jazz, avant garde, hard rock, soft rock and experimental musicians all held benefits to "save The Rud," raising enough money to keep the Pyles afloat. "It's a shame that we can't get by without help," said Ken Pyle, "but then again, these folks wouldn't have had a chance to show what incredible human beings they are."

The benefits, along with continued service of burgoo, breads and other foods, kept The Rud bumping along. But after forty years of bringing their eclectic community idea to Louisville, the Pyles decided to call it quits. In 2013, they announced they were selling the Rudyard Kipling to new owners. Ken Pyle told a reporter that the couple was "old and worn-out." He said that what had kept them going was "the love and support of the thousands of artists, musicians, poets and actors....It's been thrilling." The new owners tried to keep the restaurant going, but the Pyles' magic may have left with them, and the Rudyard Kipling closed for good in 2015.

"Keep Louisville Weird" was a thing for the Pyles long before it became a marketing slogan. Their combination of social consciousness, cooking, art and entertainment left a real legacy in the city. Perhaps they didn't leave a signature dish or create a successful franchise chain. But they may have brought about the vision Sheila created in a painting modeled after Edward Hicks's *The Peaceable Kingdom*. As Sheila put it to the *Courier-Journal*'s Bryan Woolley in 1973, "I'm pushing that you should love your neighbor as yourself and he's not a damn bit better than you are and you're not a damn bit better than him." Putting the Golden Rule into practical use—perhaps that's the real legacy of the Rudyard Kipling.

25

Squirrelly's Magic Tea Room

TRICKING LOUISVILLE INTO SAVING WHISKEY ROW

You can't open a magic place alone. You have to have a restaurant." Attorney Larry Jones—known at times as Baron LaValle and Willard Sizemore—was explaining to Vince Staten in the *Courier-Journal* why, in 1986, Salvator's by the Bridge appeared at the corner of Second and Main Streets. Bordering what was considered a sketchy row of strip clubs, roaming drunks and empty, iron-fronted shells in danger of collapse, the Italian eatery offered spaghetti sauce and strumming guitars, plus fortune-telling and the chance to go upstairs to Squirrelly's Magic Tea Room. That was where another of Jones's alter egos made handkerchiefs become walking canes, cards appear and disappear and cigarettes dance across tables. Squirrelly's show ran for fourteen years, a span that saw Whiskey Row begin changing to the vibrant area it is today—which may have been one of Jones's greatest tricks.

Lawrence L. Jones III was born in Louisville in 1926. After serving in the Merchant Marine during World War II and then in the U.S. Marines during the Korean conflict, Jones earned a law degree from the University of Virginia then came back to Louisville. He joined the law firm of Wyatt, Grafton & Sloss (later Wyatt, Tarrant & Combs). As a young man, Jones had lived in New York City. Attending old vaudeville and burlesque acts, his preteen self was "mesmerized" by the slapstick, dancing, comedy, acrobatics, animals and, of course, magic tricks. Jones haunted Tannen's Magic Shop, picking up tips from performers and buying his own tricks. He began practicing magic himself but kept it a sideline as he finished schooling, military service and law school and got married and started a family. But the young attorney couldn't give up his dreams of being a professional magician. His law partners remained skeptical. As they kept joking about his skills, Jones made a $100 bet with one partner that his act was good enough to earn an appearance on *The Ed Sullivan Show*. Taking a leave of absence from the law firm in the late 1950s, Jones took the stage in New York City as Baron LaValle. Legendary comedian Lenny Bruce was sharing the same venue and liked what he saw of Baron LaValle's act. Bruce talked to some people, and Jones won his bet with a 1961 appearance on *Ed Sullivan* with Charlton Heston, Eartha Kitt and Roger Williams. Baron LaValle made goldfish appear at his fingertips, the media-savvy Jones choosing fish that were half gold, half black so they would register on black-and-white televisions. Jones told an interviewer that "Goldfish are more delicate than doves. I had to fly to New York with them in a hatbox. Then I'd put them in the bathtub in the hotel."

In addition to winning the bet, Jones's *The Ed Sullivan Show* appearance got Baron LaValle on the children's show *Captain Kangaroo*. Jones's manager alerted him that Baron LaValle had enough engagements for a yearlong tour. But as Jones said: "They were going to send me to all the big towns. But I had a wife and three kids and I didn't want to do it. If I could have gone some place for a year, like the Folies Bergere in Paris, I would have done that." He came back to Louisville, resumed his law practice and, having proved his point, limited his magic to something he did at home. While usually serious as an attorney, especially on behalf of retired Louisville firefighters, Jones couldn't quite repress his inner trickster. At times, he would appear in the halls of his law firm dressed in overalls and fake buck teeth, pretending to be a clueless client called Willard Sizemore. He often brought a Great Dane to the office and once chose to entertain the federal court system. As attorney Greg Haynes recalled, the Army Corps of Engineers condemned some of Jones's property on Nolin Lake. Jones took pictures of himself at the property, using them to argue against the condemnation in a brief Haynes called "very touching, but absolutely meritless." Jones lost the case, but Haynes said the brief "was very clever, and it was funny....I'm sure there were some pretty hearty laughs at the federal courthouse when they saw it."

Around 1980, Jones was asked to put together a charity burlesque show and "jumped at the chance." "I'd always wanted to get myself in a burlesque house," Jones told reporter Vince Staten. "I got a stripper, a sand dancer, a singer. I did the magic, of course. It was my show." The charity event reignited Jones's desire to perform publicly. He had bought the building at Second and Main and began imagining a new magic act there. "Baron LaValle was black tie, very straight stuff, goldfish, classy,

Larry Jones performing an illusion. *Courtesy the Jones family.*

cigarettes," recalled son Stephen Jones. "But [the new persona], Squirrelly, showcased his more irreverent and naughty sense of humor. He wanted to clearly express that this was not David Copperfield or Lance Burton. This was going to be goofy." On weekends, Squirrelly began appearing in a custom-built space above the Italian restaurant. As the magician produced a lighted candle from thin air, he would utter an audible "ouch" and, as the audience tittered, would sneer: "Like to see a lawyer hurt, do you? Most people do. Know what you got when you got a lawyer buried up to his neck in sand? Not enough sand." Jones paired bawdy patter with polished, elaborate tricks in his custom-built theater.

"There was no PA system, there was no mike system. Half the show was close-up magic—his forte was sleight of hand," said Stephen, who, along with Jones's Great Dane Stormin' Norman, assisted in the show. "Everything was rigged with foot pedals. He'd play music with foot pedals. He'd do light changes with foot pedals. He didn't really need anybody until the illusions started." Jones's stage was riddled with secret panels, tunnels and triggers, with possibly the most elaborate feature being the hydraulic chair. "Every night, my first job was to find a woman in a dress, and her husband or boyfriend, and she's got to go here," said Stephen, pointing at the chair. "Because she's going up, and Squirrelly is going to look up her dress with the mirror." The massive hydraulic mechanical system, not only lifting a chair several feet but also pulling a stage rail back to protect a lady's knees, was installed just for a thirty-second gag. Other illusions included an arm-crawling silver ball and a floating, disappearing girl, usually a waitress recruited from the restaurant downstairs, who would be magically replaced by Jones's dog. And, of course, every bit of prestidigitation was accompanied by Jones's sardonic delivery.

Through the 1980s and 1990s, what was initially Salvator's, then Anthony's by the Bridge, continued to deliver decent Italian fare with musical accompaniment. On the weekends, Squirrelly reigned overhead. As one reporter put it, "There is only one place in Louisville—and possibly in the entire United States, for that matter—where you can see a magic show, have your palm read, swirl spaghetti on your fork and listen to jazz singers or a guitarist." While Squirrelly was still recruiting young ladies and their dates to his hydraulic chair, others were trying to destroy the block Jones had started to rebuild.

Once the thriving center of Louisville's whiskey economy, Squirrelly's block of Main Street had been the site not only of the original Galt House but also a variety of whiskey brokerages, barrel storehouses and blending operations. The corporate headquarters for local businesses like Brown-Forman, Belknap Hardware and the L&N Railroad Company (which Squirrelly's and Anthony's occupied) were also there. The block featured a variety of architectural styles such as the Chicago School and Revivalist, yet developers seemed determined to tear it down. Jones, however, had other plans. "The vision was there, [but] the surrounding pieces didn't exist," Stephen Jones said while discussing the plans his father had laid out before the turn of the century. Squirrelly's and Anthony's helped keep the Whiskey Row block alive, even after Jones retired Squirrelly around the year 2000 and died in 2003.

These days, Whiskey Row is a sought-after area downtown, its iron-fronted buildings bursting with development. Squirrelly no longer performs, but his theater, now known as Baron's, remains and hosts companies and events. Magic posters and memorabilia line the walls, but Main Street should remember Larry Jones for a different kind of magic: the ability to see just how good the city's future could be.

26

Taco Punk

GOOD INTENTIONS PAVING THE WAY TO ONLINE HELL

"In no way am I a racist profiteer" is probably not the best slogan for any business, let alone a restaurant. Yet somehow, Gabe Sowder found himself using this statement to defend his Taco Punk from one of the many challenges the restaurant faced, online as well as on Market Street. In its few years of existence, Taco Punk asked Louisville to embrace its sustainable, locally sourced and environmentally conscious practices, trying innovative means to keep Sowder's idea afloat. Things definitely did not go as intended.

Gabe Sowder grew up in Jeffersonville, Indiana, before graduating from Wabash College with dreams of being a writer. Instead, he found work in restaurants around the United States before returning to Louisville, getting married and spending several years working under Edward Lee at 610 Magnolia. While there, he had a vision: take the "principles of fine dining but apply them to fast food," namely tacos. Using a name his son bestowed on him after a friendly wrestling match, as "Taco Punk," Sowder started a stand at the Douglass Loop Farmers' Market and other venues, and people seemed to like his stuff. He thought about a food truck but instead opted for the 3,500-square-foot former home of Toast on Market in 2011. Sowder said everything on his menu would be made in-house using locally raised meats and sustainable seafood. Taco Punk would combine "artisan-style effort" with fast-food service. There would be tacos, tortillas, black beans, saffron rice, guacamole, queso and other standard Mexican fare.

Taco Punk sign. *Courtesy Michelle Turner.*

Taco Punk opened in January 2012 with a violet, avocado and adobe-colored interior under a grinning-skull sign seemingly inspired by Mexican Day of the Dead skulls. Things seemed to be going well. Sowder was featured in an issue of *Food & Dining Magazine* and on the television show *Secrets of Louisville Chefs Live*. In a profile, *News and Tribune* columnist Amanda Beam wrote that Sowder purchased most of his meats and vegetables from local vendors and made everything from scratch daily "using cooking techniques normally seen in fine-dining establishments." She approvingly noted Sowder's allergy- and vegetarian-conscious menu "with no additives or preservatives," as well as Taco Punk's commitment to environmental and social consciousness—composting waste, using biodegradable napkins, plates and cups, paying workers "20 percent more than the industry average" and "helping local refugees by hiring employees from that population." Sowder seemed to believe his concept would catch on, telling Beam, "It's definitely on the table for Taco Punk to expand to other Midwestern and Southern cities." In a February 2012 review shortly after Taco Punk opened, critic Robin Garr noted that "local foodies, seduced by Sowder's skills and the hipster Nulu vibe, are virtually aswoon over this recent arrival." Garr himself was excited about items like Pacific cod with a "secret chili rub," smoked beef braised in artisanal beer, crispy duck carnitas with roasted pumpkin and the "Taj-Ma-Hell," a taco with curried lamb leg, tamarind and cucumber-mint yogurt. However, while Garr enjoyed his "Yucatecan style" grilled cod taco along with grilled adobo chicken, he faulted Sowder for crumbly corn tacos and the restaurant's "too-often clueless counter service and wildly variable food and prep quality." That kind of review can hurt, but not as much as the ones arriving a few months later.

In a June 2012 opinion piece in *The Louisville Cardinal*, student journalist Rae Hodge distilled just about every criticism of Taco Punk in a piece titled "Taco Punk: Hey, Ho, Let's Go Somewhere Else." Hodge began by questioning just how "punk" charging ten dollars for a taco platter could be, and things went downhill from there. Hodge wrote that while she wanted Taco Punk to be "a culinary jewel [it] just happens to find itself in a morally dubious situation." She wanted the tacos to be so delicious she could "smile right back in the face of that giant red sugar skull that grins at me from its poster without thinking about cultural appropriation, or how racist it is to turn a Dia De Los Muertos symbol into a novelty to sell tacos." Unfortunately, after tortillas of "dry and tasteless pork" that "fell apart before reaching my mouth," Hodge wrote that she couldn't remember "the last time I paid a higher dollar-to-crap ratio for food."

The article quickly attracted media buzz, with Sowder choosing to respond on his Facebook page. "We have become accustomed to the harsh tone of the web, but Ms. Hodge's piece crossed numerous lines of decency, accuracy, and overall journalistic standards," Sowder wrote, adding, "I have eaten Latin food in many cities throughout America and Mexico and have developed a deep respect and passion for this cuisine and culture." Telling the story of how a father-son wrestling bout became a restaurant name, Sowder told "all of the haters out there who are slamming my use of the word punk" that they were "actually trashing a father's desire to connect with his son," adding that "all of you sound like a big group of bullies." Sowder's explanation continued through his logo design ("designed by our good friend Cesar Perez-Ribas [as] an homage to Latino art, not a malicious appropriation of cultural heritage"), his nonsubsidized food prices ("If you would like for my prices to drop, pick up the phone or write a letter to Rand Paul and Mitch McConnell and tell them you want family farmers to be included in the Federal Farm Bill") and his lifestyle ("I drive a crappy old car and live in a 1,000-square-foot house in Germantown"). Changing his tune from his *News and Tribune* interview, Sowder claimed that he had "no desire to see a Taco Punk in every town in America," adding that his goal was "to simply feed good people good food and have enough money to get through life and pay for my son's education."

The negative publicity (and possibly the crumbly tacos) didn't make things easier for Sowder. In January 2013, Eater Louisville website editor Zach Everson reported on Sowder's use of crowdfunding site Kickstarter. Everson framed Sowder's plea for $20,000 "to keep the doors open" as a "NuLu restaurant [asking] for donations so it can keep selling $10 taco platters." Everson opined that "The Wayside Christian Mission and Dare to Care Food Bank feed the hungry rather than charge $12.95 for the Yucatecan Style Fish Punk Platter (as tasty as it is). Might they be better places for your charitable dollars?" Sowder again defended himself, this time on WFPL-FM, citing his following Kickstarter guidelines and noting that he would have to have some "meaningful conversations" should he fail because "morals aren't cheap."

After the internet eruptions and Sowder's self-defense on WFPL, Robin Garr weighed in on the controversy. Garr noted his own early Taco Punk criticism for "spotty service" while referring to Hodge's work as "a bizarre, ranting 'review' that went viral." Hodge, commenting on the Kickstarter request, referred to Sowder as "a third-rate taco baron selling $10 papier-mâché tortillas…passing the collection plate while preaching the 'Keep Louisville Weird' sermon and serving bad beer." Garr, on the other hand, "made a small Kickstarter contribution" and revisited the restaurant, saying that his "animal-free lunch of two good-size tacos on tender, fresh-made corn tortillas" left him "very happy."

In a short time, it seemed Hodge's view had won. Eater's Everson kept Taco Punk on his "Death Watch" list, reporting on Sowder's failure to reach his fundraising goal as well as a threatened lawsuit by Louisville's Metropolitan Business Development Corporation (METCO) for nonpayment of a promissory note. (Everson later reported that, after Sowder made a payment, METCO decided not to pursue litigation.) Downtown construction clogging Market Street didn't make things any better, and by September 2014, Sowder was ready to call it quits. When Sowder announced that he was closing in October, New Albany brewer, restaurateur and contrarian Roger Baylor issued an invitation to set up at Bank Street Brewhouse across the river. Escaping north, Sowder continued to turn out tacos on weekends for a while but eventually moved on to other endeavors.

Taco Punk's efforts to supply the city with sustainably sourced Mexican food failed. Fortunately for Louisville, Bruce Ucán, a Guatemalan native who had been elevating and ethically producing amazing food before Sowder started his restaurant, continued with his Mayan Cafe.

Bibliography

Chapter 1: 732 Social

Coomes, Steve. "New Venture Brings Diners Together." *Courier-Journal*, September 20, 2008.

———. "732 Social Ends Its Run, While Garage Bar Brunch Starts Saturday." *Insider Louisville*, September 22, 2011.

Elson, Martha. "Plans for Firehouses Are Coming Together." *Courier-Journal*, December 29, 2010.

Howard, Hilary. "Louisville Neighborhood Becomes an Arts Area." *New York Times*, September 9, 2008.

Ikenberg, Tamara. "New Take on Juleps." *Courier-Journal*, April 27, 2009.

Keane, Erin. "2009 Bar Guide." *Courier-Journal*, December 16, 2009.

McMahan, Dana. "Remember 732 Social? The Gang's Getting Back Together." *Courier-Journal*, October 23, 2017.

———. "732 Social Says Goodbye." *Courier-Journal*, September 23, 2011.

Nord, Thomas. "One Great Dish: Potatoes Au Gratin." *Courier-Journal*, September 2, 2009.

Rosen, Marty. "732 Social Is a Breath of Fresh Air." *Courier-Journal*, April 25, 2009.

Chapter 2: Blind Pig

Elson, Martha. "Butchertown Makes AOL's 'Hot New Neighborhoods' List." *Courier-Journal*, September 15, 2010.

Everson, Zach. "Blind Pig Closing Saturday After Losing Eviction Case… Or Maybe It's Not Closing." Eater Louisville, October 16, 2013.

———. "Landlord's Solution Fails to Materialize: Blind Pig on Track to Shutter Saturday." Eater Louisville, October 17, 2013.

———. "Meat Owner: Liquor License Dispute with Blind Pig Behind Temporary Closure." Eater Louisville, April 10, 2013.

———. "Meat's Peyton Ray Bought the Building He Shares with Blind Pig." Eater Louisville, May 15, 2013.

———. "State Seeks to 'Revoke or Suspend' the Blind Pig's Liquor License." Eater Louisville, May 6, 2013.

Garr, Robin. "Surfin' the Bacon Bubble at The Blind Pig." *LEO Weekly*, October 20, 2010.

———. "This Blind Pig's No Visibly Impaired Porcine." *LEO Weekly*, April 14, 2010.

McMahan, Dana. "Meat Owner Floored by Bar Award." *Courier-Journal*, November 30, 2012.

———. "New Gastropub in Butchertown." *Courier-Journal*, April 10, 2010.

Ryan, Hugh. "Restaurant Review: The Blind Pig in Louisville, Ky." *New York Times*, August 4, 2010.

WDRB.com. "Blind Pig Sues Former Landlord, Business Partner." January 28, 2014.

Chapter 3: Burger Queen

Brinkley, Joel. "Candidate George Clark; Born 'With a Wooden Spoon in His Mouth,' a Self-Made Millionaire Runs for Mayor Because: 'When You Give of Yourself, You Get More Back.'" *Courier-Journal*, June 28, 1981.

Cocanougher, Kelly. "'Little League Crowd' One Key to Burger Queen's Rapid Rise." *Louisville Times*, February 1, 1974.

Fisher, Patricia. "Hoosier Woman's Burger Empire Queen." *Courier-Journal*, May 17, 1977.

Gentile, Gan. "The Historical Timeline of the McDonald's Menu." Thrillist, April 1, 2014.

Kaufman, Michael T. "J. Gordon Lippincott, 89, Dies; Pioneer Design Consultant." *New York Times*, May 7, 1998.

Kay, Joan. "Ninety Years of Special Mondays." *Courier-Journal*, November 27, 1977.

Leuke, Pam. "A Corporate Entity by Any Other Name." *Courier-Journal*, May 10, 1981.

Moeller, Philip. "A Big Piece of the Future; New Mascot, New Design." *Courier-Journal*, March 21, 1982.

———. "Druther's Looks Ahead to Life after Clark." *Courier-Journal*, December 10, 1981.

Ozersky, Josh. *The Hamburger: A History.* New Haven, CT: Yale University Press, 2009.

Thompson, Jim. "Buzzness Decision: Burger Queen Is Changing Its Name." *Courier-Journal*, November 1, 1980.

Chapter 4: Casa Grisanti

Coomes, Steve. "Nostalgia-Free Zone: Compared to Modern Restaurant Food, Casa Grisanti's Grub Was Dull." *Insider Louisville*, July 25, 2012.

Cooper, Ann. "Kentuckiana Cooks; Ice Sculptor Continues a Vanishing Continental Art." *Courier-Journal*, July 4, 1973.

Corn, Elaine. "Running a Restaurant Is a Family Affair for the Gabrieles." *Courier-Journal*, August 31, 1986.

Courier-Journal. "Artistic Plasterer, Pacifico Grisanti, Dies." September 5, 1955.

———. "Christmas Dinner; Mostly Traditional American Fare from the Grisanti Restaurant Empire's Strong-Willed Executive Chef, Frank Yang." November 15, 1981.

———. "Dorina Mattei, Co-Founder of Casa Grisanti, Dies at Age 90." January 24, 1994.

———. "Fair or Not, Fehr Is Liberty for All." January 2, 1968.

———. "Italian Restaurant Planning Grand Opening Wednesday." April 10, 1959.

———. "Mamma Grisanti Expansion Plans Scaled Back." May 11, 1985.

———. "Wine-Tasting Party Benefits Kidney Foundation." February 17, 1971.

Des Ruisseaux, Richard. "Dining at Casa Grisanti Is a Delightful Pastatime." *Courier-Journal*, January 1, 1972.

Egerton, Judith. "Dead End; Elegant Sixth Avenue Restaurant to Close Today Because It Couldn't Make Money." *Courier-Journal*, September 1, 1989.

———. "Grisanti Buys Restaurants in Chain Started by Family; Louisville-Based Owner Says Deal with Imasco Won't Involve Layoffs." *Courier-Journal*, November 16, 1989.

Ellis, Leslie. "Casa Grisanti's Standards Remain as High as Ever." *Courier-Journal*, February 18, 1983.

Finley, John. "Casa Grisanti Does It with Care." *Courier-Journal*, January 2, 1981.

Gabriele, Vincenzo. "Downtown: Let's Hustle to Make It Better." *Business First*, October 30, 2003.

Garr, Robin. "Casa Grisanti: Service to a Fault." *Courier-Journal*, October 29, 1988.

Gregg, Cissy. "Chicken Cacciatore." *Courier-Journal*, March 13, 1955.

Kaukas, Dick. "Seasoned Diplomat; Grisanti's Tact—and Luck—Put Him at Top of Restaurant Business." *Courier-Journal*, August 10, 1987.

Massey, Steve. "4 Grisanti Restaurants Sold to Spur Expansion." *Courier-Journal*, November 16, 1984.

———. "Officer Leaves Grisanti Division; Plans for More Restaurants Delayed Again." *Courier-Journal*, September 30, 1985.

Neely, Paul. "Mamma' Gives Good Value for the Price." *Courier-Journal*, December 8, 1978.

Roby, Jack. "Fare Comment: Vincenzo's." *Courier-Journal*, December 5, 1986.

Shafer, Sheldon. "Casa Grisanti to Lay Down Its Napkin, Close Saturday." *Courier-Journal*, May 7, 1991.

———. "Ex-Grisanti Partner to Operate Humana Restaurants." *Courier-Journal*, May 30, 1986.

———. "Old Louisville Apartment Building, Casa Grisanti Renovation Approved." *Courier-Journal*, November 20, 1984.

Song, Kyung M. "Casa Grisanti Rise and Fall Guided by Passion for Fine Dining." *Courier-Journal*, May 20, 1991.

Stanwell, Ann. "Can Louisville Change Its 'Steak and Potatoes' Image?" *Courier-Journal*, November 26, 1972.

Tompor, Susan. "Grisanti to Buy 19 Restaurants in 8-State Chain." *Courier-Journal*, July 8, 1987.

Ward, Joe. "Casa Grisanti Expanding Outside Louisville Area." *Courier-Journal*, July 9, 1983.

———. "Grisanti Firm Prepares to Open American-Cuisine Restaurant." *Courier-Journal*, January 26, 1981.

———. "The House of Grisanti: A Two-Generation Tale of Fine Louisville Food." *Courier-Journal*, September 23, 1979.

Chapter 5: Club Grotto

Coomes, Steve. "Club Grotto Closes with Sale Pending." *Courier-Journal*, August 15, 2009.

Courier-Journal. "2000 Dining Guide." November 4, 2000.

Fritschner, Sarah. "Marvelous Mozzarella." *Courier-Journal*, August 28, 1998.

Karman, John R. "Parents Keep Jim McKinney II's Club Grotto Cooking Following His Death." *Business First*, October 7, 2002.

Mikulak, Ron. "Try This at Home." *Courier-Journal*, August 17, 2005.

Reigler, Susan. "Cave in and Try Magical Club Grotto." *Courier-Journal*, January 18, 1997.

———. "A Rewarding Pilgrimage." *Courier-Journal*, June 16, 2001.

———. "Tastes Blend in a Sea of Influences." *Courier-Journal*, January 15, 1994.

Rosen, Marty. "Amid So Many Bitter Ends, 6 Sweet Successes!" *Food & Dining Magazine*, Summer 2004.

Chapter 6: Corbett's

Coomes, Steve. "Corbett's Sale of Equus and Jack's Lounge Was Timely and Wise." *Insider Louisville*, May 28, 2018.

———. "With His 'Point Made,' Chef Dean Corbett Sells Produce Company to Creation Gardens." *Insider Louisville*, March 30, 2013.

Courier-Journal. "Dean Corbett" (obituary). October 15, 2018.

Everson, Zach. "5 Questions with Chef Dean Corbett." Eater Louisville, December 4, 2012.

Fritschner, Sarah. "Dinner à la Equus." *Courier-Journal*, January 18, 1987.

Gregory, Kathryn. "Remembering Chef through Best Recipes." *Courier-Journal*, October 16, 2018.

Jones, Michael L. "Chef Deano Remembered at Sold Out Taste of Corbetts." *Food & Dining Magazine*, February 22, 2019.

Mariani, John. "Esquire Best New Restaurants, 2008." *Esquire*, October 10, 2008.

Menderski, Maggie. "Corbett, Chef behind Equus & Jack's, Has Died; He Spurred Development in the Brownsboro Road Area." *Courier-Journal*, October 14, 2018.

Otts, Chris. "Corbett's Promises Fine Dining among Chains." *Courier-Journal*, January 16, 2008.

Rosen, Marty. "Corbett's Exudes Excellence." *Courier-Journal*, March 29, 2008.

Chapter 7: Dobbs' Luau Room

Courier-Journal. "Polynesian Restaurant Sues Another over 'Luau' Name." May 20, 1961.

Ex-Louisvillian. "Hawaii, Paradise of the Pacific: Life in Honolulu and Much Interesting Information About the Troublesome Little Republic." *Courier-Journal*, July 25, 1897.

Finley, John. "A Rarity: An Airport Restaurant That Has Really First-Class Food." *Courier-Journal*, October 5, 1979.

Hershberg, Ben Z. "Restaurant at Standiford May End Its Lunch Service." *Courier-Journal*, September 15, 1983.

———. "Standiford's Luau Room to Close, Citing Sharp Decline in Business." *Courier-Journal*, October 13, 1983.

Miller, David. "Aloha! Polynesian Restaurant Returns to Louisville." *Louisville Skyline*, July 10, 1985.

Roby, Jack. "Fare Comment: Luau Room." *Courier-Journal*, September 20, 1985.

Ruark, Robert. "He Went Back to Beach-Combing and Became a South Sea Babbit." *Courier-Journal*, January 4, 1950.

Stuart, Will. "Lee Terminal Size to Be Doubled; Construction Will Start by July 1; Polynesian Restaurant Set." *Courier-Journal*, March 17, 1959.

Thierman, Sue McClelland. "Lanai and Luau Bring Influence of Polynesia To Lexington Hotel." *Courier-Journal*, October 18, 1959.

Chapter 8: Downstairs at Actors

Courier-Journal. "ATL Restaurant Named 'The Starving Artist.'" March 21, 1974.

Kay, Joan. "Palate and Palette Get Pleasing Attention in Museum's Cuisine." *Courier-Journal*, July 12, 1981.

Roby, Jack. "Fare Comment." *Courier-Journal*, March 7, 1986.

Chapter 9: Embassy Supper Club

Advertisement reference to "Scene after dark" by Richard Des Ruisseaux. *Courier-Journal*, May 7, 1972.

Des Ruisseaux, Richard. "Obituary for Sam Pedro Fell Short." *Courier-Journal*, May 31, 2000.

Ellis, Leslie. "The Embassy Supper Club Treats Patrons Diplomatically—and Then Comes the Check." *Courier-Journal*, April 1, 1983.

Neely, Paul. "Elegant, Safe but Certainly Not Exotic." *Courier-Journal*, September 1, 1978.

Shatkin, Elina. "Lawry's the Prime Rib: The Story of an L.A. Icon." DiscoverLosAngeles.com.

Chapter 10: El Camino

BonAppetit.com. "America's Best New Restaurants 2014: The 50 Nominees Are Here!"

Coomes, Steve. "El Camino Will Feature a Tiki Bar, Authentic Street Food and a Mexican Bakery." *Insider Louisville*, September 11, 2012.

Downs, Jere. "Mexican Food." *Courier-Journal*, June 15, 2016.

Loosemore, Bailey. "El Camino Finds New Space in Germantown." *Courier-Journal*, February 5, 2017.

McMahan, Dana. "The Dish." *Courier-Journal*, July 24, 2014.

Rosen, Marty. "Fiesta Fantastic, El Camino Takes Food and Surroundings to Creative Heights." *Courier-Journal*, November 7, 2013.

Chapter 11: Essex House

Courier-Journal. "Essex House Suit Settled by Compromise." February 11, 1969.

———. "In the Path of a Wider Watterson." May 6, 1973.

———. "Lawsuit Splits Brother-Owners of Essex House." May 22, 1968.

———. "'Pancake House' Set in Old Lumberteria." March 30, 1960.

———. "Widening the Watterson May Take 380 Homes." November 27, 1980.

Finley, John. "Essex House: Specialty Is Fun, Not Food." *Courier-Journal*, March 28, 1980.

———. "Jury Orders Sawyer, Short to Pay a Total of $10,000." *Courier-Journal*, February 25, 1971.

Hardy, Kay. "Letter to the Editor." *Courier-Journal*, May 18, 1980.

Thompson, Jim. "Sap's Foods Selling the Essex House." *Courier-Journal*, May 23, 1971.

Tunnell, James S. "Sawyer Suit in Court After Months of Rumor." *Courier-Journal*, August 14, 1969.

Chapter 12: Hillbilly Tea

Black, Jane. "The Next Big Thing in American Regional Cooking: Humble Appalachia." *Washington Post*, March 29, 2016.

Bowling, Caitlin. "Hillbilly Tea Closed for Good, Not Just the Holidays." *Insider Louisville*, December 29, 2016.

Coomes, Steve. "Post Mortem on Hillbilly Tea No. 4: It Never Should Have Opened." EatDrinkTalk.com.

Courier-Journal. "Funtown Mountain Attractions." April 1, 2015.

Downs, Jere. "Hillbilly Tea Abruptly Closes; Owner Plans to Focus on Similar Eateries Elsewhere." *Courier-Journal*, May 12, 2015,

Kaufman, Steve. "'Karter Louis-ville': Hillbilly Tea Entrepreneur Multi-Tasking on Expansion, New Concepts." *Insider Louisville*, June 8, 2011.

McMahan, Dana. "Hillbilly Tea Opening Soon." *Courier-Journal*, May 1, 2010.

———. "Hillbilly Tea Prepping Baxter Outpost." *Courier-Journal*, September 25, 2014.

———. “Hillbilly Tea Returns to Downtown Louisville.” *Courier-Journal*, January 21, 2016.

———. “Hillbilly Tea Team to Open Appalachian Sushi Restaurant.” *Courier-Journal*, February 26, 2015.

———. “Hillbilly Tea to Add Space and Alcohol.” *Courier-Journal*, March 5, 2011.

Rosen, Marty. “Country Cookin’ Done Right.” *Courier-Journal*, July 24, 2010.

———. “No Reservations.” *Courier-Journal*, July 10, 2014.

Sisk, Remy. “A Hillbilly Revival.” *LEO Weekly*, October 3, 2016.

Chapter 13: The Hangouts of Harrods Creek

Castner, Charles B., and S. Tinsley Campbell. “‘Fog Bound Five’s’ Origin.” *Courier-Journal*, July 13, 1975.

Courier-Journal. “Casting Club to Meet.” April 17, 1941.

———. “Electrical Problem Apparently Started Blaze at Chick Inn.” December 18, 2002.

———. “Kessler Gets Roadhouse Permit.” April 4, 1956.

———. “Parsons Fires 643, Young 629.” February 25, 1947.

———. “Restaurant, Bar on River Road Gutted by Fire.” March 10, 1977.

———. “Restaurant Rezoning Still Faces Opposition; Panel Backs Change for River Creek Inn.” July 26, 2002.

———. “River Creek Inn Owner Is Charged with Murder.” July 27, 1997.

———. “Zoning Board Refuses to Withhold Permit for Community Building.” December 22, 1943.

Davidson, Shannon. “Chick Inn Destroyed by Fire.” WAVE3.com, December 17, 2002.

Eaton, Yvonne. “Marvelous Marble; Cool Stone Is Hot Look Again in Interiors.” *Courier-Journal*, April 18, 1985.

Garr, Robin. “There’s Nothing Stingy About Cheap Eats at These Two Family Restaurants.” *Courier-Journal*, June 20, 1987.

Howington, Patrick. “An Era Is Over.” *Louisville Times*, March 10, 1977.

Loosemore, Bailey. “History & Nostalgia: The Pine Room Is Breathing Life Back into the Tiny Town of Harrods Creek.” *Courier-Journal*, May 5, 2019.

Lundy, Ronni. “Down by the Riverside.” *Courier-Journal*, September 1, 1990.

Rush, Ken. "Hunter, Parsons Named to Hall of Fame," *Courier-Journal*, September 29, 1985.

Schaver, Mark. "Man Killed on River Road during Bar Burglary Attempt; Police Say Owner Evidently Justified in Shooting Man." *Courier-Journal*, July 25, 1997.

Schneider, Grace. "Harrods Creek; Settlers Took a Turn at Mills; Verdant Hills and Lowlands Were Home to Diverse Groups." *Courier-Journal*, November 1, 1989.

Shafer, Sheldon. "Department Store Rezoning Supported." *Courier-Journal*, May 20, 1977.

Voice-Tribune. "John 'Bus' Parsons" (obituary). May 17, 2017.

Wade, Scott. "River Creek Inn Gets Ready for New Era; Flood-Ravaged Site to Reopen on Harrods Creek." *Courier-Journal*, June 24, 1998.

———. "River Creek Inn's Renovation Is Still on Hold." *Courier-Journal*, December 30, 1998.

———. "River Creek Inn Work Gains Clearance." *Courier-Journal*, March 2, 1999.

Chapter 14: The Islands/Splash

Courier-Journal. "Builder Al Schneider Dies at 86." May 28, 2001.

———. "Islands Opened Door for Newport." November 18, 1987.

———. "Mayfly Horde Invades Riverfront." June 22, 1988.

———. "Residents Wrestle with Goo Dropped by River." December 29, 1990.

Garr, Robin. "Fine Food Almost Made Up for The Islands' Flaws." *Courier-Journal*, January 9, 1988.

———. "The Islands Loses Gary Flynn." *Courier-Journal*, December 10, 1988.

Hill, Bob. "The Islands and the Trolley: Of Eyesores and Illusions." *Courier-Journal*, December 5, 1987.

Kifner, John. "An Oasis of Casinos Lifts a Poor Mississippi County." *New York Times*, October 20, 1996.

McDonough, Rick. "Floating Restaurant Opens amid Continued Controversy." *Courier-Journal*, December 6, 1987.

———. "A Friendship Stranded on The Islands." *Courier-Journal*, October 29, 1987.

———. "Judge Sides with Islands in Louisville Dispute." *Courier-Journal*, November 6, 1987.

———. "Owner Says Islands Suit Blocking Sale to Investor." *Courier-Journal*, August 27, 1988.

———. "Restaurant Barging into Louisville." *Courier-Journal*, November 26, 1987.

O'Doherty, Mary. "Curious Crowds Tickled Pink to Peek at Islands." *Courier-Journal*, November 27, 1987.

PRNewswire.com. "'Father of Mississippi Gaming' Richard J. Schilling, Jr. Dies at 62." January 30, 2010.

Shafer, Sheldon. "Owner Hopes Voyage of Splash, The Islands Puts Them in the Pink." *Courier-Journal*, February 18, 1992.

Chapter 15: Jim Porter's

Bradby, Marie. "Throngs Roll into Porter's, Rock Back the Clock." *Courier-Journal*, September 10, 1981.

Coady, Jean Howerton. "Special Memories Reserved for Seelbach." *Courier-Journal*, October 17, 1977.

Courier-Journal. "Board of Aldermen, Friday Evening, March 23." March 26, 1855.

———. "Coffin Had to Be Built for Porter; He Died 100 Years Ago Tomorrow." April 24, 1959.

———. "Death of James D. Porter, the 'Kentucky Giant.'" April 26, 1859.

———. "A Giant's Home." June 2, 1895.

———. "Rogers Has Purchased Walnut Restaurant." July 24, 1971.

———. "Town Brevities." May 22, 1856.

Gregg, Cissy. "Giant Jim Porter's Tavern 'Reborn' Here." *Courier-Journal*, October 12, 1957.

———. "New Cookbooks Tell Tastes of Teen Boys and Diners Out." *Courier-Journal*, September 9, 1959.

Neely, Paul. "If Only the Food Matched the Service." *Courier-Journal*, December 15, 1978.

Puckett, Jeffrey Lee. "Jim Porter's Returns with a New Name, and a New Emphasis on Entertainment." *Courier-Journal*, April 7, 1990.

Shafer, Sheldon. "Renovation of Seelbach Will Get Louisville's Aid." *Courier-Journal*, November 30, 1977.

Wells, Wayne. "Restaurant to Get New Name, Look." *Courier-Journal*, September 29, 1989.

Chapter 16: Kienle's

Courier-Journal. "After Dark." Advertisement quoting Richard des Ruisseaux in *Louisville Times*. April 28, 1974.

Elson, Martha. "Tabling Its Service: Kienle's Delicatessen Will Shut the Doors Soon." *Courier-Journal*, March 25, 1992.

Garr, Robin. "Great Ethnic Eats." *Courier-Journal*, December 10, 1988.

Roby, Jack. "Kienle's Proves That Good Things Do Truly Come in Small Packages." *Courier-Journal*, August 17, 1984.

Simmons, Ira. "At Kienle's, You Have It Their Way." *Courier-Journal*, February 25, 1978.

Chapter 17: Lentini's Little Italy

Courier-Journal. "Bankruptcy Petition Filed." May 5, 1961.

———. "The Sound and the Fury." April 4, 1974.

———. "Tornadoes Rip Kentucky, Indiana; 117 Killed, Damage in the Millions." April 4, 1974.

Cutler, Gayle. "Lentini's Rises from the Ashes; Restaurant Reopens After Fire—Again." *Courier-Journal*, April 26, 1989.

Garr, Robin. "Still Hearty After All These Years." *Courier-Journal*, October 7, 1989.

Green, Marcus, and Amy Bafumo. "Snapshots of People at Work Re: Phat Thanh Le." *Courier-Journal*, June 9, 2003.

Muhammad, Larry. "The Dish." *Courier-Journal*, November 9, 2001.

Neely, Paul. "Dinner at Lentini's: Honest; Unaffected." *Courier-Journal*, February 2, 1979.

Ratterman Brothers Funeral Home. "Gasper Lentini" (obituary).

Reigler, Susan. "Old Favorite Makes for Roman Holiday." *Courier-Journal*, November 5, 1997.

Rosen, Marty. "Cafe Mimosa Makes a Good Move." *Courier-Journal*, January 23, 2010.

———. "Dinner at Da Vinci; Lentini's Outpost Served Up Disappointing Fare." *Courier-Journal*, October 20, 2007.

———. "New Jarfi's Bistro Transforms Lentini's." *Courier-Journal*, May 10, 2008.

Chapter 18: Lynn's Paradise Cafe

Baxter, Missy. "Lynn's Celebrates Sixth Anniversary." *Courier-Journal*, July 31, 1997.

Broder, John M. "Bill Clinton: 'Dumb Politics' to Discount Fla. and Michigan." *New York Times*, May 20, 2008.

Columbo, Alice. "Cook's Corner." *Courier-Journal*, October 18, 1995.

Courier-Journal. "Dining Out." October 25, 1991.

Downs, Jere. "Lynn's Building Sells; Items to Go." *Courier-Journal*, April 10, 2016.

———. "Lynn's Paradise Cafe Sold; Everything Must Go." *Courier-Journal*, March 25, 2016.

Eaton, Yvonne. "A Little Piece of Paradise; Lynn Winter Lives and Works Amid Cheerful, Kitschy Clutter." *Courier-Journal*, January 20, 2015.

Egerton, Judith. "Owner Chooses New Site for Lynn's Paradise Cafe." *Courier-Journal*, September 4, 1993.

Fernandez, Maisy. "Lynn's New Store Is Full of Swirly Fun Things." *Courier-Journal*, December 10, 2003.

Fritschner, Sarah. "Mac & Cheese from Paradise Makes It to Oprah's 'Best.'" *Courier-Journal*, February 19, 2003.

Heilenman, Diane. "American Style features Paradise Cafe." *Courier-Journal*, March 30, 1997.

Lundy, Ronni. "A Taste of Paradise." *Courier-Journal*, August 24, 1991.

Lynch, Caroline. "In a form of cobranding, small businesses share space." *Courier-Journal*, December 29, 2003.

Martinez, Natalia. "Tensions over Lynn's Paradise Cafe Reach Boiling Point." WAVE3.com, January 20, 2015.

Mikulak, Ron. "Chicken Dishes Back in Favor." *Courier-Journal*, July 7, 2010.

Morgan, Veda. "Ugly Lamp Contest Makes Light of Beauty." *Courier-Journal*, August 30, 1998.

Neuhauser, Ken. "The Best Bet: An A-maize-ing Mural at Lynn's Paradise Café." *Courier-Journal*, November 14, 1997.

———. "Cafe Is Home for Derby Fest-O-Rama." *Courier-Journal*, May 2, 1997.

———. "Kentucky Derby Party Comes to Paradise (Cafe)." *Courier-Journal*, May 3, 1996.

Nold, James. "Talking Up Down-Home." *Louisville Magazine*, July 1992.

Reigler, Susan. "Fun and Babes in Louisville." *Courier-Journal*, May 16, 2002.

———. "Lynn's Gets New Chef." *Courier-Journal*, April 3, 1993.

———. "Lynn's Is Still Paradise." *Courier-Journal*, July 2, 1994.

———. "Lynn's Paradise Cafe Lauded in *Bon Appetit*." *Courier-Journal*, August 23, 2002.

———. "Whooooooz!" *Courier-Journal*, September 2, 2000.

———. "World of Swirl at Lynn's Paradise Cafe." *Courier-Journal*, December 19, 2003.

Rosen, Marty. "Lynn's Cafe Aces Breakfast." *Courier-Journal*, September 13, 2008.

WAVE3.com. "Lynn's Paradise Cafe Accused of Abusing Workers, Unfair Policies." January 11, 2013.

WLKY-CBS 32. "Ugly Lamps Out for This Year's Kentucky State Fair." July 13, 2013.

Chapter 19: Min's East End Cafe

Bulleit, Paul. "Bean Stringing Champ Retires." *Courier-Journal*, August 10, 1973.

Courier-Journal. "Min's Cafe Closed; Former Owner Says He May Reopen It." January 25, 1989.

Chapter 20: Mozz

Coomes, Steve. "Ambitious Mozz Restaurant to Open Breeder's Cup Week." *Insider Louisville*, September 8, 2010.

———. "Cautionary Tale: Investor Reveals the Madness behind Mozzaria Meltdown." *Insider Louisville*, December 6, 2012.

———. "Finally, Mozz Closes and Antonovich Is Once Again Gonetonovich." *Insider Louisville*, September 14, 2012.

———. "Mozz Co-owner Opening Mozzaria May 2 in Red Star Tavern Location." *Insider Louisville*, April 25, 2012.

———. "News Stew: Mozz Voted Best New Spot…." *Insider Louisville*, July 6, 2011.

Fritschner, Sarah. "Fast Lane." *Courier-Journal*, April 11, 1990.

Insider Louisville. "Court Docs: Mozzaria at 4th Street Live Was in Trouble Nearly as Soon as It Opened." August 15, 2012.

Miller, Nancy. "Really Cool Dining Downtown." *Courier-Journal*, November 27, 2010.

Chapter 21: Myra's

Corn, Elaine. "Hail to the Hamburger." *Courier-Journal*, May 23, 1984.

Courier-Journal. "Mervyn C. Rinker" (obituary). March 22, 1983.

———. "Myra L. Rinker" (obituary). March 24, 1988.

Ellis, Leslie. "Formally Myra's Is Better Than It Was Formerly." *Courier-Journal*, July 2, 1982.

Elson, Martha. "Lots of Memories in Store." *Courier-Journal*, March 19, 2008.

Finley, John. "New Myra's Has Its High Points." *Courier-Journal*, December 5, 1980.

Garr, Robin. "Deitrich's in the Crescent Is a Winner." *Courier-Journal*, December 3, 1988.

Gregg, Cissy. "New Kind of Cheesecake Also Draws the Adjectives." *Courier-Journal*, June 29, 1949.

Chapter 22: Normandy Inn

Courier-Journal. "Ex-restaurant Owner Dies." June 2, 1983.

Des Ruisseaux, Richard. "Dream Restaurant." *Courier-Journal*, March 25, 1972.

Jaehnig, Walter. "Normandy Hotel to Become Colorful Pub, Restaurant." *Courier-Journal*, March 12, 1967.

McGrath, Meredith. "He's Not Your Average Trucker." *Louisville Times*, July 20, 1974.

Neely, Paul. "Normandy's Promises Remain Unfulfilled." *Courier-Journal*, October 27, 1978.

Chapter 23: Parisian Pantry

Colombo, Alice. "Cook's Corner." *Courier-Journal*, October 22, 1986.

Courier-Journal. "Pantry Changes Owners." September 15, 1990.

Duerr, Sandra. "Mom, Son Carve Niche with French Restaurant." *Courier-Journal*, January 5, 1987.

Garr, Robin. "Bread Saves the Day at Parisian Pantry." *Courier-Journal*, September 2, 1989.

———. "Cafe, Pantry Cook Up Some Changes." *Courier-Journal*, May 21, 1988.

Holland, Holly. "French Restaurant Files Bankruptcy Petition." *Courier-Journal*, February 26, 1988.

Kaukas, Dick. "Fresh Bread Is Hot; French Finesse Has Transformed Baker Jean Yves-Joret into a Rising Star." *Courier-Journal*, April 14, 1992.

Lundy, Ronni. "Charming, but Inconsistent." *Courier-Journal*, September 28, 1990.

Otolski, Greg. "Stress of Running a Restaurant Spurs Closure of Parisian Cafe." *Courier-Journal*, August 31, 1995.

Reigler, Susan. "Potholes on the Road to Paris." *Courier-Journal*, February 25, 1991

Roby, Jack. "Parisian Pantry Is Nice, but Man Does Not Live by Bread Alone." *Courier-Journal*, July 27, 1984.

Scanlon, Leslie. "Additions and Renovations Bring 'Sparkle' Back to Bardstown Road." *Courier-Journal*, February 12, 1984.

Simmons, Charitey. "Kitchen Tour May Cook Up Locust Grove Supporters." *Courier-Journal*, March 4, 1987.

Chapter 24: The Rudyard Kipling

Courier-Journal. "Key Players." September 4, 2014.

———. "Mulloys Will Sing, Speak." March 10, 1968.

———. "The Pick of the Bluegrass." May 26, 1974.

———. "War Zone 'Poverty.'" February 16, 1970.

Hill, Bob. "Pick Your Decade and Pass the Beer at the Rudyard Kipling." *Courier-Journal*, March 10, 1990.

Kaukas, Dick. "The Rud." *Courier-Journal*, February 1, 1985.

O'Neill, Tom. "Rudyard Kipling Changing Hands; Owners of That Place on Goss to Redo Kitchen." *Courier-Journal*, December 12, 2013.

Puckett, Jeffrey Lee. "Out to Save The Rud." *Courier-Journal*, March 28, 2003.

———. "The Rud Rocks Again." *Courier-Journal*, January 14, 2000.

Pyle, Sheila Joyce. "Did Dolly Parton Cheat This Woman's Man?" *Courier-Journal*, February 26, 1978.

Roby, Jack. "Fare Comment: Rudyard Kipling." *Courier-Journal*, May 2, 1986.

Shallcross, Mark. "Worried About Not Fitting In? Drop in at The Rudyard Kipling." *Courier-Journal*, November 12, 1987.

Stewart, Leslie. "Ken Pyle." *Louisville Music News*, August 2003.

Woolley, Bryan. "Maybe You Can Go Home Again." *Courier-Journal*, February 18, 1973.

Chapter 25: Squirrelly's Magic Tea Room

Burba, Paula. "Lawrence Jones III, Attorney, Magician, Dies After Illness." *Courier-Journal*, August 27, 2003.

Jones, Maggie. "The Magician's Daughter." *Nieman Reports*, Fall 2012.

Staten, Vince. "Lawyer Transforms Self on Stage of Tearoom." *Courier-Journal*, December 18, 1987.

Chapter 26: Taco Punk

Beam, Amanda. "Unique Take on Tacos: Jeffersonville Native's Locally Focused Mexican Restaurant Celebrates One Year." *News and Tribune*, January 29, 2013.

Bowling, Caitlin. "Taco Punk Moving into New Albanian's Kitchen." *Business First*, December 1, 2014.

Clouser, Stephanie. "Chef Gabe Sowder Leaves 610 Magnolia to Open Fast-Casual Taco Joint." *Business First*, January 27, 2012.

Downs, Jere. "Taco Punk in NuLu Closing." *Courier-Journal*, September 23, 2014.

Everson, Zach. "From the Death Watch Notebook." Eater Louisville, February 8, 2013.

———. "METCO Sues Taco Punk for $33,000." Eater Louisville, February 26, 2013.

———. "Taco Punk'd: NuLu Restaurant Asks for Donations So It Can Keep Selling $10 Taco Platters." Eater Louisville, January 23, 2013.

———. "Taco Punk Says METCO Lawsuit 'Will Not Move Forward.'" Eater Louisville, March 8, 2013.

Garr, Robin. "Dining: The Small Stuff Punks Taco Punk." *LEO Weekly*, February 22, 2012.

———. "Kick (Re)Start Taco Punk? Sure, Why Not?" *The Voice-Tribune*, February 20, 2013.

Hodge, Rae. "Taco Punk: Hey, Ho, Let's Go Somewhere Else." *The Louisville Cardinal*, June 7, 2012.

Sowder, Gabe. "'Rae Hodge, Businesses Such as Taco Punk Are Revitalizing a Wasteland into a Vibrant Neighborhood.'" *Insider Louisville*, June 13, 2012.

Thompson, Ashlee Clark. "Undeterred by Critics, Taco Punk Kickstarter Campaign Continues." WFPL, January 25, 2013.

Index

N

O

P

Q

R

S

T

V

W

Y

Z

About the Author

An award-winning author and brand strategist, Stephen Hacker enjoys history, cooking and chickens. His restaurant experience spans waiting tables, testing menu items and creating advertising campaigns as well as writing reviews for local, national and international publications, including *Louisville Magazine* and Eater. Along with his spouse, Michelle Turner, he is the author of *Lost Restaurants of Louisville.*